"The authors have succeeded in providing a practical roadmap for people struggling with OCD to incorporate mindfulness into their CBT treatment. For many, this will be the addition that makes all the difference."

—**Diane Davey, RN, MBA**, program director, OCD Institute

"*The Mindfulness Workbook for OCD* is a unique must-have companion to enhance the standard application of ERP treatment for both therapists and individuals living with OCD. The authors' compassion is evident throughout, and reflects a deep understanding of the suffering that OCD imposes every day. Chapter by chapter, the authors demystify the concepts of mindfulness in a very user-friendly manner. The workbook-style approach allows the reader to mindfully examine the ways in which OCD has formed its hold, and provides concrete exercises for loosening that hold and regaining a life and identity free from OCD. I am excited to recommend this book to my clients and colleagues alike."

—**Kathleen M. Rupertus, PsyD**, clinician, The Anxiety and OCD Treatment Center, Delaware

"As someone who has benefitted greatly from both cognitive behavioral therapy *and* mindfulness practice, I am thrilled to see a book showcasing how powerful their pairing can be for those of us with OCD. The practical roadmap Jon Hershfield and Tom Corboy provide here offers turn-by-turn directions to the one place OCD simply can't survive: the present moment!"

—**Jeff Bell**, author of *Rewind, Replay, Repeat: A Memoir of OCD*

"A valuable addition to the self-help library of all OCD sufferers, as well as those who treat OCD! The book presents state-of-the art information for incorporating very effective mindfulness techniques into effective OCD treatment."

—**Lee Baer, PhD**, author of *Getting Control* and *The Imp of the Mind*, and clinical professor of psychology at Harvard Medical School

"The concept of mindfulness is proving to be an increasingly important concept in dealing with a number of disorders, and this book ably extends it to OCD. It presents a concise and practical approach to this topic, with straightforward easy-to-follow instructions. The skills readers will gain from learning to be fully in the present moment and accepting what is occurring there will surely add a great deal to their efforts at overcoming what is a confusing and painful disorder."

—**Fred Penzel, PhD**, psychologist and executive director at Western Suffolk Psychological Services, Huntington, NY

"Although mindfulness plays a critical role in coping with the uncertainties of OCD, practical how-to help for sufferers and clinicians wasn't there. Hershfield and Corboy's workbook masterfully fills this void with details of how to employ mindfulness techniques for all the different ways OCD manifests itself."

—**Jonathan Grayson, PhD**, director of the Anxiety and OCD Treatment Center of Philadelphia

"This is a wonderful and very well-written book, full of lively and helpful examples. It will be a huge help to those with OCD and related illnesses. The book gives very useful and practical tools to manage the symptoms of OCD. This is a major contribution that will help patients immensely."

—**Michael A. Jenike, MD,** professor of psychiatry at Harvard Medical School

"This is the most comprehensive, straight forward, easy-to-follow treatment manual combining CBT and mindfulness-based techniques. For those who may not have access to treatment providers, *The Mindfulness Workbook for OCD* will be an excellent resource to help guide and navigate how to overcome their obsessions and compulsions in a succinct, clear manner. By far, the best addition to my resource library and referral list."

—**Robin Zasio, PsyD, LCSW,** author of *The Hoarder in You* and featured doctor on the television show, *Hoarders*

The
Mindfulness
Workbook
for OCD

A Guide to Overcoming Obsessions AND Compulsions Using Mindfulness AND Cognitive Behavioral Therapy

JON HERSHFIELD, MFT · TOM CORBOY, MFT

NEW HARBINGER PUBLICATIONS, INC.

Distributed in Canada by Raincoast Books

Copyright © 2013 by Jon Hershfield and Tom Corboy
New Harbinger Publications, Inc.
5674 Shattuck Avenue
Oakland, CA 94609
www.newharbinger.com

Cover design by Amy Shoup
Acquired by Jess O'Brien
Edited by Nelda Street

Library of Congress Cataloging-in-Publication Data

Hershfield, Jon.
  The mindfulness workbook for OCD : a guide to overcoming obsessions and compulsions using mindfulness and cognitive behavioral therapy / Jon Hershfield, MFT, and Tom Corboy, MFT.
    pages cm
  Includes bibliographical references.
  ISBN 978-1-60882-878-4 (pbk. : alk. paper) -- ISBN 978-1-60882-879-1 (pdf e-book) -- ISBN 978-1-60882-880-7 (epub) 1. Obsessive-compulsive disorder. 2. Cognitive therapy. I. Corboy, Tom, 1957- II. Title. III. Title: Mindfulness workbook for obsessive-compulsive disorder.
  RC533.H468 2013
  616.85'227--dc23
                              2013037197

Printed in the United States of America

20   19   18

15   14   13   12   11

To Shannon, Emma, and Sadie: thanks for making the present so worthwhile. And to OCD sufferers everywhere: you are stronger than you think.

—Jon Hershfield, MFT

For Shanti: thank you for being the best thing that ever happened to me.

—Tom Corboy, MFT

Contents

PART 3
Mindfulness, OCD, and You

Foreword

The history of mindfulness and its inclusion in cognitive behavioral practice is long and complicated. As a concept and practice, mindfulness is most closely associated with Buddhism; but it actually has roots in many traditions, and a place in everyone's experience. As a component of treatment, mindfulness first showed up in stress management and, later, pain management, pioneered by Jon Kabat-Zinn. Marsha Linehan incorporated mindfulness into the treatment of borderline personality disorder in her groundbreaking development of dialectical behavior therapy. Mindfulness became an important part of work with recurrent depression in mindfulness-based cognitive therapy for depression by Zindel Segal and other therapists in the field.

I first learned the potential importance of mindfulness in CBT while learning about DBT and MBCT. However, when I first discussed it with some highly respected experts on OCD, I was met with some dismissive responses and strange looks. My intention to broach the subject of mindfulness in a self-help book I was cowriting led to a conflict with coauthors that threatened the project. Some of the early attempts to usher the benefits of mindfulness into working with OCD were awkward, which may have fed resistance. The best thinking in science comes from people who are open to new ideas and, while skeptical, are simultaneously willing to look at the data. We have arrived at a point where it's generally recognized that mindfulness is an important component of well-conceptualized CBT for OCD.

I have known Jon Hershfield for a number of years, primarily from his participation in an Internet support group for people with OCD. He could tell his story of how OCD has affected his life and led him to become a therapist, focusing on helping others with this common and often devastating disorder. We will have to wait for his next book to hear that story, but we can all benefit from what he learned. Jon Hershfield and Tom Corboy are well known for their work with people who are suffering with OCD. In this self-help workbook, Jon and Tom describe how to include mindfulness in a self-help approach to managing OCD. First they provide a clear and understandable explanation of mindfulness and ideas about basic practice. They then skillfully blend ideas about how to practice mindfulness with solid CBT for OCD. I often hear people with OCD complain that the self-help books they read don't describe OCD in the way that they experience the disorder, so they wonder if others have the same symptoms that they do or if they really have OCD. Because OCD is one of the most diverse diagnoses, no book can realistically cover all the possible presentations. There are chapters devoted to many of the more common ways in which OCD presents so that readers can easily identify with the symptoms and learn how to use CBT, including mindfulness practice, to help themselves. Additionally the examples and ideas about how to integrate mindfulness into CBT for a variety of OCD presentations will give therapists a head start in helping their clients.

I look forward to recommending this book to my clients with OCD and to other therapists.

—James Claiborn, PhD, ABPP, ACT

Introduction

Welcome to *The Mindfulness Workbook for OCD*. Although this book is not a substitute for professional treatment, you can use it as an adjunct to treatment, with or without a therapist's guidance, if you wish to incorporate mindfulness concepts into your approach to better mental health in the presence of obsessive-compulsive disorder (OCD).

Who Are We?

When I was age twenty-eight, a lifetime of struggling with a myriad of OCD issues came to a head, and I realized I simply couldn't go it alone anymore. I made two decisions that would change my life forever. I sought treatment from an OCD specialist, and I began writing about OCD. My therapist taught me to challenge my usual way of processing information. This involved the hard work of combining cognitive therapy, behavioral therapy, and acceptance of discomfort into a larger approach to overcoming the grip my disorder had on me.

The platform I chose for writing about OCD was an online discussion board. On this board, I met Michael Jenike, James Claiborn, and Jonathan Grayson and started picking up on their ideas about cognitive behavioral therapy (CBT) and mindfulness—things like not assuming that your thoughts are important just because you have them, or that uncertainty is intolerable just because it's uncomfortable. Also, my fellow sufferers who found the words to articulate their OCD experiences online inspired me such that I wanted to give back more than an e-mail could offer. With the amazing support of my wife and my parents, I was able to shift life's gears and obtain a master's degree in clinical psychology.

After Tom Corboy hired me at the OCD Center of Los Angeles, I knew I was in the right place when the materials he was presenting to clients endorsed the very core concepts that had helped me on my journey: cognitive behavioral therapy and mindful acceptance. It all kept coming back to that, combining the clinical approach of CBT with the more personal, introspective approach of mindfulness.

In my time there, I was blessed with the opportunity to work face-to-face with OCD sufferers, the kind of people whose stories I previously had encountered only in writing. There were so many different stories, yet all said the same things about how thoughts and feelings are hard to accept *as they are*. Between clients, I wrote blog articles about patterns I noticed and what was working in treatment, and Tom published them on the OCD Center of Los Angeles website. These writings drew the attention of Jess O'Brien at New Harbinger, because he recognized the demand for a mindfulness book specifically about OCD. Jess's willingness to take a chance on an unpublished author, as well as his tireless efforts to bring this project to the public, is why this book exists.

I am humbled by the opportunities I've been given in recent years to directly help people overcome their OCD, to be a part of a community of OCD therapists with the same passion, and to write this book as I continue my own journey from both sides of the therapist's desk.

—Jon Hershfield, MFT

I was introduced to the concepts of mindfulness and acceptance from an altogether unexpected source. In 1989, my father casually suggested that I read M. Scott Peck's book *The Road Less Traveled*. I had never heard of it and was immediately struck by its first three words: "Life is difficult" (Peck 1978, 15).

That's quite an opener. But what followed was even more challenging: "Once we truly know that life is difficult—once we truly understand and accept it—then life is no longer difficult" (Peck 1978, 15).

I wasn't quite sure what to make of this idea. Having had a typical midwestern childhood, I had been raised to believe that difficulties were to be faced and conquered. I had never even remotely entertained the notion that I should accept the difficulties life threw at me, and I wasn't at all sure I liked the idea.

In the early 1990s I attended graduate school for counseling psychology at the University of Southern California, where I wrote my thesis on the treatment of OCD. By then, research had become conclusive that the most effective OCD treatment was cognitive behavioral therapy. Then, while I was working as a postgraduate intern in Los Angeles, a client noted that she had found a measure of peace in a book by Pema Chödrön titled *The Wisdom of No Escape* (1991), which focused on the benefits of mindful awareness and acceptance of the pains and discomforts inherent to the human experience.

Well, sometimes the student is the teacher. I bought a copy of the book and was immediately taken aback by the clarity of its logic. Chödrön's basic thesis was that our discomfort would diminish if we just stopped trying to deny and avoid our unwanted thoughts and feelings, and instead chose to mindfully accept and even learn from them.

In the following years, I sought and read many more books that focused on mindfulness and acceptance. In 1999 I founded the OCD Center of Los Angeles, a private outpatient clinic specializing exclusively in the treatment of OCD and related anxiety-based conditions. Since then, our treatment program has been focused entirely on the integration of traditional CBT with the principles of mindfulness and acceptance.

In 2009 I met Jon Hershfield when he applied for a position at the center. It was obvious that Jon was bright and motivated, and soon thereafter I hired him for a postgraduate internship. It immediately became apparent that Jon had a profound understanding of the complexities of OCD. What's more, I have been consistently impressed by his seemingly effortless ability to integrate CBT with mindfulness and acceptance principles, both clinically and in his writing. Simply put, he completely gets it.

This book is meant to be used as a workbook; it presents a hands-on approach to OCD based on melding traditional CBT techniques with the somewhat-more-abstract "meta" principles of mindfulness and acceptance. It's my sincere hope that this book helps you to more mindfully experience and accept whatever life throws at you.

—Tom Corboy, MFT

About This Book

The aim of this book is to discuss how a concept called "mindfulness" can be used to treat obsessive-compulsive disorder in combination with a type of treatment called "cognitive behavioral therapy." The gold standard of treatment for OCD, CBT has been demonstrated to significantly and effectively reduce symptoms (Houghton et al. 2010). In fact, even "brief intensive cognitive behavioral therapy (CBT), using exposure and response prevention, significantly improves obsessive-compulsive disorder symptoms in as little as four weeks" (Saxena et al. 2009). An exploration in combining mindfulness with CBT found that "far from undermining the process, mindfulness complements or even enhances [CBT]" (Fairfax 2008). In the pages ahead, we will explore some of the main tools used in CBT and how implementing mindfulness can contribute to treatment.

This book has three parts. Part 1 focuses on developing a basic understanding of three modalities: mindfulness, cognitive therapy, and behavioral therapy, which come together in *mindfulness-based cognitive behavioral therapy* (MBCBT). You will familiarize yourself with the main tools of each modality for responding to OCD: mindful awareness, challenging distorted thinking, and exposure with response prevention (ERP).

Part 2 breaks down common obsessions found in OCD and describes how to use the tools learned in part 1 to address them. This includes fostering a better understanding of how OCD uses each triggering thought or feeling to push you into responding compulsively. You will examine the different types of distorted thinking that each obsession promotes and specific tips for doing exposures. Each chapter also includes tips on guiding your thought process using meditation while being challenged by your obsession.

Part 3 explores the other details of living with OCD and using mindfulness to maintain healthy relationships as an OCD sufferer. There you will also find recommendations for treatment resources.

Take a Breather

Reading about OCD when you have OCD isn't always easy. At times throughout this book, you may find yourself getting triggered, or "spiked," by its concepts. Take in the information at whatever pace feels appropriate for you. Challenge yourself to let the book present itself, but allow yourself whatever space or breaks you need to get through it. There's no prize for finishing this book in one sitting. We hope that your gaining the tools and strength to fight your OCD will be the real prize.

PART 1

Mindfulness and OCD

Obsessive-compulsive disorder is a psychiatric and psychological mental health issue with an estimated lifetime prevalence of 2.3 percent (Ruscio et al. 2010). An *obsession* is an unwanted, intrusive thought. This type of thought may present itself as an idea, image, impulse, urge, memory, or other internal information, and you experience it as unwanted and distressing. A *compulsion* is a behavior designed to reduce or avoid the discomfort that comes from your experience of an obsession. This behavior may be physical, such as washing or checking, or mental, such as reviewing or neutralizing. We will discuss these terms in more detail in upcoming chapters.

Disorder describes something that's not contained or not as stable as it should be. It's out of order: *disordered*. The presence of an obsession or a compulsion is not enough to diagnose someone with obsessive-compulsive disorder. For the condition to be considered a disorder, you have to experience impaired functioning, reduced quality of life, and lost time from attending to your obsessions and compulsions.

Your OCD Story

If you've ever read a workbook on OCD or any related disorder, you've probably seen case examples presented as "Bob's story," "Mary's story," and so forth. You may have read their stories and thought, *That's me!* Your story is unique because it happened to *you*. But for the most part, all OCD stories are your story.

One day, you had a thought that didn't seem right to you. It didn't reflect your belief. But it was *your* thought. Why would you have it without believing it? This disconnect triggered a *feeling*—not just mild dissatisfaction but some kind of psychological pain. Like any healthy, rational person, you set out to get rid of that pain. However, everything you could come up with seemed to help only for a brief moment and then caused the pain to strike back more viciously.

The more you tried not to think about it, the more the thoughts intruded. The more you self-soothed, the more you hurt. The more you avoided, the more you were forced to confront things. You tried to let go but couldn't. People said, "Just drop it," and you began to resent them for being unfair. Your world got smaller and smaller, the things you love became reminders of what you hate, and you began to see yourself as an imposter.

When you see yourself as the imposter, you perceive yourself as merely pretending to be a functioning human being; inside you experience constant, relentless suffering. The imposter is contaminated, a danger to others, deviant, unloved, disconnected, imperfect, immoral, and, above all, not in control.

You're not just anxious. There's something sharp jabbing into your mind. But all is not lost. Although your suffering may be great, your ability to change this experience is within your grasp.

CHAPTER 1

The Brain, the Mind, and You

Take a moment to consider your present reality as involving three separate entities: your brain, your mind, and *you*.

The brain is a physical collection of organic matter that resides in your skull. Like other organs in the body, it serves a variety of functions through a complex series of chemical and electrical interactions. One of the main functions of the brain is to organize data. This includes thoughts, feelings, and physical sensations. The brain presents this data similarly to how a computer presents zeros and ones to a processor.

The mind is that processor. It receives the data and acts on it in a variety of ways. It works on the data. It filters it, promotes it, rejects it, and adds color and meaning to it.

You are simply you. You are the one who goes by your name and the one watching what the mind is doing with the data it receives. You are your "being," your person.

Most of us have great difficulty separating ourselves from the mind. If the mind is analyzing the meaning of a thought, then it seems as if we are personally responsible for that analysis. Mindfulness is a concept grounded in the idea that you can observe what your mind is doing and decide for yourself how involved you want to be in the process.

In his book *The Mindful Brain*, Daniel Siegel (2007, 5) describes the mind as "a process that regulates the flow of energy and information." So whether it's helpful for you to imagine the mind as part of the brain or as part of something more ethereal, consider that what we are mostly interested in is what it *does*, not what it is. What we are attempting to understand here is how the mind interacts with the OCD brain and with you, the OCD sufferer.

The Basic Concept of Mindfulness

Mindfulness is the state of acknowledging and accepting whatever is happening in the present moment exactly as it is. As a skill, it emerges from your developing the ability to notice what your mind is doing with the information it receives from the brain. This involves noticing individual acts of the mind, as well as patterns and tendencies of the mind. The practice of mindfulness for OCD is the cultivation of a relationship between you and your mind, in which you cooperate with one another in your battle against the disorder.

The experience of OCD is feeling very much out of control of your mind. When you don't see yourself as separate from your mind, you may feel as if *you* are doing whatever your mind is doing. That means you not only are being asked to cope with the presence of intrusive thoughts that come with your OCD, but also are taking on personal responsibility for how terrible they appear. You may attempt to pull the mind away from the unwanted thoughts by purposefully reviewing and predicting horrific hypothetical situations, trying to convince yourself that what you came up with would never happen, that you're safe and it's okay for your mind to stop. But it doesn't work. The brain presents, the mind receives and acts, and you feel like a slave to the whole process.

But if you develop the capacity to better observe what the mind is doing, you can begin to view the OCD thoughts as something different from their content. Because those of us with OCD so often find pain in OCD thoughts, we become accustomed to seeing our minds focused on judgment and rejection of what the brain offers. Rather than let the mind take in the thoughts, feelings, and physical sensations as they are, we fight. But it's the wrong fight. If you can choose to stay on the sidelines and observe what your mind is receiving and where it tends to go with it, you can begin to choose measured responses to your OCD thoughts. Instead of automatically reacting as when two chemicals spontaneously change form, you can begin to *respond*. To react to OCD is to jump into compulsions. To respond to OCD is to observe what your mind is doing and choose your next step.

Staying in the Present

If you've read any mindfulness books or done any meditation, you've probably heard about staying in the present. At first, this may seem a bit silly, and you may think, *How can I be anywhere but the present? I'm here, right now. I'm here, right now, completely freaking out, because I think I may have touched something I wasn't supposed to an hour ago, which means that in a week or two, I'm going to find out I caught a disease! Right now is awful!*

But that isn't right now. That's your OCD's twisted version of right now. It is, in fact, the past, which no longer exists, and the future, which exists only in theory. In other words, it's the "what *if*," not the "what *is*," that OCD lives in. In the "what is," there's no material for the OCD to work with. You are just a person reading a book, looking at words right now. Even *thinking* can be done in the present. Okay, you are a person *thinking*. There's nothing there for the OCD to get its claws into. However, in the "what if" is the fear of what might have happened or what might happen still. Then there's the urge to *do* something about that fear, to keep it from being realized. That is compulsion.

Another way of looking at this is to consider that mindfulness is about keeping your mind close to your body. Your body is sitting in a chair with this book. Your mind is there with you, reading these words. When your mind wanders off to replay a conversation you had last week or to think about an upcoming event, then your mind is nowhere near your body. In that space is where OCD presumes ownership of the mind. Can you think of a situation in which you often find your mind traveling to the past or the future instead of staying where you are in the present?

Accepting what's going on right now, being truly mindful, doesn't necessarily mean feeling at peace. You may feel anxious right now. What *is* may mean that right now, where you sit, as you are, you do not know when or if the thoughts, feelings, and sensations you are experiencing will ever go away. Only in the present can you look at that without judgment and potentially experience it without fear.

Thoughts Are Thoughts, Not Threats

The primary difference between people with OCD and those without it is not simply the content of the thoughts, but their perspective on the thoughts. If your perspective is that a particular thought is "bad" in and of itself, then that thought may become problematic. A number of factors can influence how a thought becomes "bad." When you are in a totally relaxed state, a thought about snapping and doing something crazy may seem unworthy of attention, like junk mail. In an anxious state, that same thought may seem like a terrible indictment or warning of a nightmare to come: *If this is in my head, I have to get it out!*

If you can imagine your thoughts as a line of train cars, people with OCD and other anxiety disorders tend to keep stopping the train to make sure everyone has a ticket. Mindfulness asks that you simply observe the train as it passes. You're only at the station on your way to work. You don't have to involve yourself in ticketing and making sure the right people are on the right trains. This means acknowledging that unwanted thoughts are occurring, but not evaluating those thoughts as being particularly meaningful. Instead of changing what the thought means, you are changing your perspective toward the thought and how you process the fact that the thought is occurring. It's not happening *to* you. It's simply *happening.*

Thoughts as Words

Another way of considering the notion that thoughts are thoughts, not threats, is to look at how you view words. When you see a word, you call it the thing that it relates to. In his excellent workbook *Get Out of Your Mind and Into Your Life*, Steven Hayes (2005) describes how the mind is made up of a network of "relational frames" in which concepts are experienced internally as things they relate to. When you experience an OCD thought, you are also being made aware of all the things to which you relate that thought. For most thoughts, this doesn't trouble you, but for thoughts, feelings, and sensations that you associate with your disorder, you perceive the obsession as something of greater value than it really is. It's not just the obsession, but also all things that you associate with it.

Practice: Here's a practice in noticing how the mind works. Look at the following word.

MIRROR

Ask yourself, *What is this?* Well, it's a mirror. Right, it's a mirror. However, if you stared at this page and tried to do your hair or makeup using it, we would consider this a bit odd. You don't see your reflection in the preceding mirror. So it's *not* a mirror. It's the *word* "mirror."

But is it the word "mirror"? Yes and no. We call it a word, but "M-I-R-R-O-R" is really a string of letters in a specific order that makes us think of a word that we relate to a reflective glass surface, called a "mirror." In a different order, it would just be a bunch of letters. "MRRIOR" doesn't mean much. And what are letters anyway?

Just symbols, little drawings to which we have agreed to assign a certain value. This is an "M," this is an "R," and so forth.

So a series of meaningless symbols is given meaning and then put in an order that *adds* to its meaning. This series of symbols is now called a "word," and this word triggers an idea. This idea triggers images—in this case, of a reflective surface—and all related thoughts, feelings, and sensations that accompany an awareness of being near a reflective surface.

If you have OCD, experiencing an unwanted thought is as if you opened this book and an actual mirror fell out onto the floor. The thoughts are presented as having *intrinsic* value, *automatic* importance, and *urgent* relevance to some behavioral response. Mindfulness practice suggests that you view the thought in much the same way as you look at words. They are empty vessels that are given power after the mind organizes and considers them. The thought of being contaminated isn't the same as *being* contaminated. It's a *thought* of it.

Feelings Are Feelings, Not Facts

Feelings are basically thoughts about physical sensations. You get a lump in your throat, tightness in your chest, sweaty palms, and dry mouth, and then you call it something: guilt, for example. You say, *That means guilt. I am guilty.* Then your OCD pushes you to explain the presence of guilt rather than accept it as it is. So you begin an endless journey of trying to figure out what crime you committed that could justify such guilt, until you eventually come up with something to blame the guilt on. But the relief is short-lived, because feelings are *feelings*. They are not facts. They are not fingerprints. They are just ideas about physical experiences. Like thoughts, they are born empty and are given meaning through behavior.

If you live with OCD, it's likely that you often wake up feeling *guilty* and spend your day investigating yourself and trying to find a way of appropriately sentencing yourself for the crime. Or maybe you just feel that something is *off*. What's the first feeling you become aware of when you wake up? Describe it here:

_____

_____

_____

_____

OCD demands that you look at these feelings and sort them out, put them in some kind of neat, tidy box to be shipped off and destroyed. The OCD threatens you with severe punishment, the severest of all: the idea that your feelings signify who you are, that guilt means you are a criminal, and that fear means you will be annihilated. The OCD says that these feelings are problems and that you must fix them or suffer.

Mindfulness practice invites you to shrug your shoulders at the OCD and say, *Well, that's a feeling*. Experience the feeling as a *feeling*, a thing that comes and goes in the body and provides little useful information about who you are or what you will do.

Sensations Are Sensations, Not Mandates to Act

The greatest mindfulness challenge for the OCD sufferer is to respond nonjudgmentally to physical sensations. For the health-anxiety sufferer, every pain is a sign of a serious illness and an indicator of supreme irresponsibility for allowing it to exist. For the person with sexual obsessions, every tingling sensation in the groin is viewed as proof of deviant orientation and predatory predisposition. So physical sensations trigger feelings, which trigger thoughts, and they all converge in your mind like waves crashing on the shore.

Mindfulness asks that you view physical sensations just as you see thoughts and feelings. They are *experiences*. Pain is pain, and we can all agree that it feels bad. But if you let it feel bad and leave it at that, you maintain clarity. Clarity is what enables you to see the difference between a headache and a brain tumor. In other words, see physical sensations as what they *are* and observe your urges to define them as what they *could be*.

The Spotlight

The problem with OCD isn't that you think too much. It's that you confuse the intensity, volume, or visibility of your thoughts with their importance.

The Average Mind

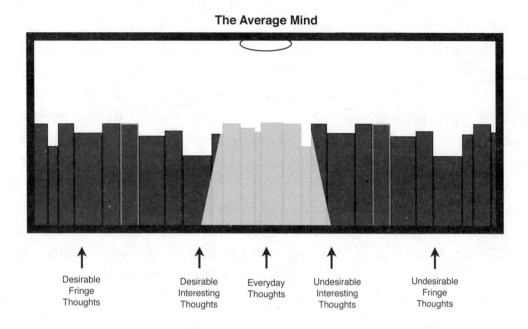

Look at the image above. It's a shelf with books on it. The books are all lined up in a row, each with its own purpose and design, each full of information, facts, theories, memories, and stories. Yet at the end of the day, each is just a book. The books are different from one another yet the same.

Above the books is a spotlight. It shines down within a certain spectrum of light, brightly illuminating the books in the center, somewhat illuminating the books to either side of its beam, and leaving what may or may not be additional books obscured on both ends of the shelf.

The brightly lit books in the middle are your regular, everyday thoughts. You accept them at varying degrees of importance but largely without any judgment. They are the thoughts that the sky is blue, that it's time to go to the bathroom, that pretzels are salty, and so forth. Whether or not you have OCD, you are aware of these types of thoughts, and they are regularly present in your consciousness.

Where the spectrum of the spotlight fades at either end, we encounter more of our "interesting" thoughts. They may be interesting and desirable, or interesting and undesirable. You might think about getting a bonus at work on the left side of the spectrum and about being audited by the IRS on the right side of the spectrum. These are thoughts that draw your interest when you are aware of them. These interesting thoughts may be exciting or upsetting. They may be the dark and creepy thoughts that we all have but don't admit to having. They may be the joyful and often-juvenile thoughts that we also all have and rarely admit to having. The average person has these thoughts readily available but must turn his attention toward them to take notice of them. Because these thoughts are only partially lit, they aren't presented to the mind in the same way that everyday thoughts are.

Reviewing the graphic, you can see that farther out along the right side of the shelf are our undesirable "fringe" thoughts. This is where thoughts about death, extreme irresponsibility, peculiar sexual or aggressive notions, and so forth reside. The average person has these thoughts. Occasionally the thoughts appear uninvited. Usually they have to be dug for. If you ask someone to think of something disturbing, maybe for a creative-writing project, she might dig here to see what comes into her consciousness. If you tell someone to come up with a wacky idea for a birthday present or a pitch for a horror movie, this is where she will go in the mind to find them. These thoughts are more than interesting: they are *out there*.

Past this dimly lit spectrum, there may still be many "books" to read, but the average non-OCD person is unaware of them. If he isn't being prompted to dig for these edgy, deep fringe thoughts, he might need to be reminded by something he saw on the news to bring them into present consciousness.

Many people will claim not to have any of these thoughts. They'll say things like, "I've never *thought* of turning my wheel into oncoming traffic." But to say the words necessary for making this statement, you are, by default, having these thoughts! It's not that the non-OCD person doesn't have such thoughts; she does. She simply doesn't register her awareness of these thoughts as problematic. She doesn't ask why or when the thoughts are there, and thus doesn't process that they *are* even there.

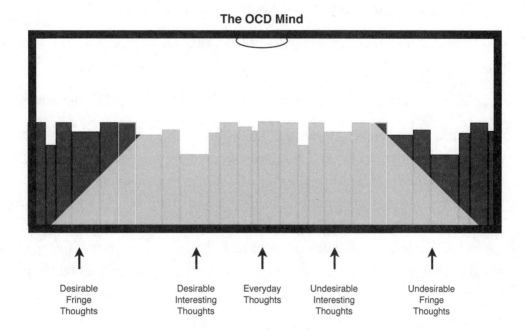

The OCD Mind

↑ Desirable Fringe Thoughts

↑ Desirable Interesting Thoughts

↑ Everyday Thoughts

↑ Undesirable Interesting Thoughts

↑ Undesirable Fringe Thoughts

Look at the graphic above. This is the OCD mind. Notice the range of the spotlight. The *interesting* and *fringe* thoughts are just as brightly lit as the everyday thoughts. They are not more meaningful, just more brightly lit. Here are some typical thoughts that may be lit up in the OCD mind but are left obscured at the edge of the shelf in the non-OCD mind.

The last person to touch this bathroom stall may have had a disease; I may have touched it, so I might now have a disease.

I am not disgusted by a man with his shirt off, so I could be so deep in the closet that even I don't know I'm gay.

My not taking the fourth step on these stairs, but only the third one, will trigger a series of events that will end in the death of an innocent person.

Mom will die if I don't say the word "healthy" right now.

When I picked up my infant daughter, my hand touched her backside. I might be a child molester.

I didn't pull the parking brake hard enough, so my car will roll away from the curb and hit a child.

I have left the stove on, which will burn down the house. My cat will be burned alive.

That kitchen knife is sharp. I could suddenly grab it and stab my husband.

That pedestrian is no longer in my rearview mirror. I may have hit him with my car without noticing it.

Thinking about my blinking will make me blink weirdly forever, and I'll go insane.

In our experience, if you get more than a handful of OCD sufferers in a room, most of them will look at the previous list and acknowledge that at one point or another, they were aware of having some of these fringe thoughts. Maybe the thoughts never became full-fledged obsessions, but they presented themselves. And these people weren't trying to be clever. The thoughts just popped into their heads. Take a few moments to list some of your disturbing *fringe* thoughts here. They don't have to be related to your primary obsession. What thoughts emerge at the surface of your mind that you think belong far deeper down?

_____

_____

_____

_____

_____

Now try the same with *fringe* thoughts from the *positive* side. These thoughts may be related to curing cancer, winning the lottery—you name it. Be a superhero. Let these thoughts be just as insane as the ugly, scary ones you obsess about. Notice how hard this is. We all tend to think of our positive fringe thoughts as silly and not worth much attention. What would the OCD experience be like if we applied the same emphasis on our negative fringe thoughts? Write your more desirable fringe thoughts here:

_____

_____

_____

_____

Perhaps you wish you could narrow the spectrum of your spotlight: *know less* of what goes on in your mind. Mindfulness suggests that to remove the need to reduce the spectrum of the spotlight, you simply acknowledge that brightly lit thoughts are not more important just because they are more noticeable. After all, the volume of a person's voice doesn't correlate to the importance of what he is saying. The size of the font in the word "MIRROR" a few pages back didn't make the word any more like an actual mirror. The intensity of the thoughts, feelings, or sensations you experience need not correlate to their value.

The Broken Dam

Try to imagine your mind as a village. Picture a valley floor with little huts, people, livestock, roads, and lots of streams of water, like veins connecting one area of the village to another. It's a pretty happy place but complicated, requiring a lot of attention and cooperation among its villagers.

The valley is surrounded by steep mountains and, on one side, a huge dam, larger than the imagination. On the other side of this dam is the largest body of water in the universe. It contains all thoughts that are possible to have—all thoughts. *What's the weather like in Santa Monica today? There are 31,622,400 seconds in a leap year.* Therein are all thoughts that anyone could ever have who has ever had a thought—including the thoughts you like, the thoughts you don't care about, *and* the thoughts you hate.

Now, because the village (your mind) needs water (thoughts) in order to function, there are lots of carefully placed holes in the dam that allow for a steady stream of desirable input. This water lands safely on the village floor and goes through all of the necessary streams and aqueducts for the village to thrive. For the most part, the dam holds everything back. It separates you from your thoughts. Your mind couldn't handle being aware of all thoughts at all times. Most of what goes on in the mind is a complete mystery. All you really need are some basics, just a consistent trickle of certain thoughts so that you can tie your shoes and brush your teeth.

But when you have OCD, there are some cracks in the dam such that extra water comes leaking through. The barrier that separates your *wanted* thoughts from the rest of your thoughts seems to be doing a subpar job. It's not a *bad* job. Otherwise your mind would be "flooded" all day. But it's not as effective as it could be.

You can view this unwanted stream of thought as the definition of an obsession. It's intrusive, it's undesired, and you perceive it as problematic. Your first response to it may be to climb the dam and plug the cracks with something. Or in the heat of anxiety, you may find yourself just taking a hammer to it. But this never works. At first, doing so may appear to slow the leak, but soon the crack gets bigger and the stream of obsessive thoughts gets more intense. This is why acting on compulsions doesn't work.

Mindfulness isn't about stopping the flow of unwanted thoughts. It's about seeing the dam. It means taking a moment to notice that although most things are working as you expected, there *are* in fact some cracks in the dam and there *are* in fact some intruding streams of thought. This leaves you with two options: pound your fists against the dam, hoping this stops the leak, or accept the leak as simply something that *is*. Maybe you can use the extra water in your mind to better irrigate the crops of your mind. Or maybe this water has no specific use and you need to learn to live in a wetter climate. In the end, there's only acceptance. Let the thoughts in. Let them mingle with the other thoughts. Let them simply *be*, and accommodate them by changing your perspective on the value of their presence.

Framing the presence of unwanted thoughts as just the added flow of particles to a larger body of water takes away the importance of identifying them as *good* or *bad*. It creates space for you to view the thoughts as mere thoughts, without judgment and without your having to *do* anything about them.

Meditation: The Practice of Mindfulness

You don't have to meditate to relieve your OCD. Still, you might want to meditate, and it might help. Meditation, in its simplest form, is literally *practicing* mindfulness. It's setting aside time, from a single moment to several hours, to stop resisting the *present* experience and to simply notice it. All basic sitting and breathing meditation really means is that you are attending to sitting and breathing only and that anything else is temporarily less important for you to attend to. This "anything else" includes thinking, solving problems, figuring things out, mentally reviewing, analyzing, and so forth.

Whenever you become aware of something other than sitting and breathing, you acknowledge it and then return to sitting and breathing. Basically, you are practicing mindfulness by practicing *not minding* whatever happens to be going on internally or externally as you sit and breathe.

Breathing meditation is such a common form of meditation, because breathing is one thing that we always do, that's always present, and that's always real. There's nothing theoretical about breathing, so when you think about your in-breath and your out-breath, by definition you must be in the present.

The present is a magnetic anchor that you are clinging to. Your OCD is constantly trying to pull you away from that anchor, away from the "what is" into the realm of the "what if." Meditation is simply noticing when you've been pulled away, allowing for that pull, and then gently guiding yourself back.

Gentleness is actually important here. If you judgmentally call yourself back to the present with thoughts like *Think about your breath! Stop obsessing! You can't do anything right!* the meditation won't work. This only pulls you further away from the present and into the judgmental stance the OCD thrives on.

This *guiding back*—using your awareness of your mind to acknowledge when you've left the breath and purposefully bringing yourself back *to* the breath—is an exercise in the same way that push-ups are an exercise. Returning to the present is an *ability* and, as such, something that can be strengthened with practice. Even a little practice makes you stronger in this regard. What you are practicing is the *coming back*. You may have noticed that many times when you are in the throes of an obsession, you ask yourself to stop: to come back from the review and just let things be. You try, but the runaway mind ropes you back in. By practicing anchoring yourself to the present in meditation, you can improve your ability to return from an obsession even when you are not meditating.

When you have OCD, being in the present may hurt, whereas letting your compulsions pull you away may spell relief. The OCD has a way of turning the very concept of meditation into its opposite. It doesn't mean you can't meditate because of your OCD. It means you have to allow for the OCD when you choose to meditate. You may be thinking about the times you've tried meditation in the past and come across these bits of resistance:

Sitting quietly with all these thoughts in my head is too painful. I won't last thirty seconds.

If I sit and breathe for five minutes, that's five minutes of being unproductive, and I'm not okay with that.

I've tried, and I can't do it right. I just get bored and annoyed with myself.

I keep thinking and ruining it.

Use this space to jot down any reasons you think using meditation as a tool against OCD might be challenging for you:

_____

_____

_____

_____

_____

A Basic Breathing Meditation Practice

Sit in a relaxed position in a chair, on a couch, or somewhere else that's comfortable. Plant your feet and rest your hands at your sides. *Don't* clear your mind. It's a waste of energy, and it can't be done anyway. Instead, start observing how your mind is *full*, and let it be that way for now.

Close your eyes and breathe in through your nose. Then exhale through your mouth. If you are unfamiliar with diaphragmatic breathing, try to imagine the air going through your nose and then down through a tube to your stomach, not to your lungs. When you inhale, let your stomach expand. This is sometimes called deep breathing, not because it involves particularly large breaths, but because it's deep in your body. If this is too odd for you, breathe as you normally would, but the advantage to diaphragmatic breathing (or belly breathing) is that it gives you something else to connect to as you breathe. It's a part of the breathing process and thus a wider target for your attention. It also keeps your shoulders from rising as much when you inhale, which helps keep your body in a more relaxed position. But do whatever you want this time around, because this *concept* is actually more important than doing meditation "right."

When you exhale, imagine your stomach deflating like a balloon. As the breath passes your lips, notice the vibration, the temperature, and anything else about the out-breath. You may find it helpful to make a "wind" sound as the air leaves your body. This can help make the breathing more intentional, making it an even wider anchor for you to stay present with.

However slowly you start to breathe, try to slow down your breathing even more. One of the things you are accomplishing by breathing slowly and intentionally is modulating the way the brain receives oxygen. When we panic, we hyperventilate, because the brain is telling the body that it needs energy to fight or run from something horrible. We give the brain energy by pumping it with short bursts of oxygen. This is why people are sometimes asked to breathe into a paper bag when they are hyperventilating; this forces them to re-inhale their own carbon dioxide, thus depriving the brain of oxygen and relaxing it. Pacing your breath in meditation helps put your brain in a more relaxed state. Although this may feel good, it's really secondary to the point of all of this, which is that in your relaxed state, you are better able to practice mindfulness.

If you've ever wondered why cigarette smokers find smoking to be relaxing when nicotine is a stimulant, the answer is not just because it quells their addiction. When you smoke a cigarette, you inhale and exhale, slowly and with intention. And you do this paced breathing for roughly seven minutes. If you took a break from work, went outside, and just pretended to smoke a cigarette, you would see the results (and without the smoke!).

Almost immediately after sitting and making the conscious decision to meditate, you might notice that your OCD is out to get you. You become aware of all your uncomfortable thoughts and feelings, plus annoying thoughts about how meditation itself is simply peculiar. You may feel distracted by anxiety, stomach discomfort, dizziness, a thousand unreachable itches around your body. The tendency is to see these things as blocking you from meditating.

Mindfulness would suggest that you see these things not as distractions, but simply as experiences. The thoughts, feelings, and physical sensations are just happening. Notice them and practice not minding. Respond to each and every one of them with a nonresponse: *Hey there, thought-about-such-and-such, that's okay. I don't mind your being here, but I'll go ahead and return my attention to the breath for now.*

Maybe you'll find this easy; maybe it won't work at all. That's fine. It's all fine, because all we're practicing is acceptance and present-mindedness. Maybe immediately after this meditation, you'll go right back to problem solving and dealing with your OCD. But for now, for the next few minutes, let yourself act differently. Let yourself not mind.

After a minute or two of pacing your breath and practicing returning to it whenever something grabs hold of your attention, you can stop. That's a short form of meditation. You basically just stayed present and practiced not taking the bait from your OCD. Maybe now you're already engaging in compulsions, but at least you put in the effort to try something different for a few minutes. Tomorrow, do it again. Maybe during the process, you had five actual seconds of relief from OCD problem solving. Maybe next time you'll have seven seconds. Or maybe, more importantly, next time you become aware of an obsession about the past or future, you will come back to the present that much quicker.

A Progressive Muscle Relaxation Meditation

If you want to meditate some more today, add this version of progressive muscle relaxation. Progressive muscle relaxation was first developed in 1934 by Edmund Jacobson, whose research demonstrated that systematic release of tension in the muscle fibers represented the opposite physiological response to anxiety and, thus, was effective in reducing anxiety states (McCallie, Blum, and Hood 2006). This is typically performed by purposely tensing and releasing muscles, but in this exercise, focus on release without tension to avoid the potential of getting stuck in a physically tense position.

What you will do for the remainder of the exercise is to continue the paced breathing while visualizing breathing *into* various parts of your body. You can think of this as some sort of wellness scanner in a science fiction movie that's set in the future: a device is passed along the body, and as it passes each part, it removes some tension.

Picture a line floating above your head, like a little cartoon halo. What you'll do is imagine breathing into this line and pushing it down across your body. When the unwanted thoughts and feelings start tugging at you, do the same as you did before: simply respond to them, *Okay, I hear you, but right now I'm going to attend to this thing instead.*

Once you have a clear image in mind of this line above your head, take a nice, slow breath into it. And as you exhale, imagine the line passing over your scalp, your eyes, your nose, your cheeks, and your lips and then stopping just above your chin. As it passes over this part of your body, imagine that it takes with it some of your angst, some of your tension, even some of your OCD. Let yourself notice any sensations that might occur in your earlobes, your eyelashes, and so forth.

Let yourself attend to where this imaginary line is resting, and how everything above it feels just a little more relaxed than everything below it, which has remained unchanged. When you are in doubt, or if you become confused or lost during the meditation, just nod politely to your confusion and return to the breath.

Now go again, breathing into that line and lowering it as you exhale. Let it pass by the muscles and bones in your neck, and let it rest just above your shoulders.

Imagine the individual tendons in your neck letting go. Let your head lean forward a bit if it helps make it more real for you. Let yourself be aware of how the entirety of your head and neck is just a little lighter, somehow a little different from the rest of your body.

Breathe into that line and lower it down across your shoulders and chest. Let the line stop at your elbows and rest just above your belly. Imagine your shoulders dropping, as if your arms could just slide off. Feel that knot in your chest that the OCD is constantly messing with, and acknowledge whether it has loosened up at all. Notice how your biceps and forearms feel different from one another, separated by the imaginary line of attention.

Breathe into that line and lower it again, now across your belly to your waist, down your wrists and hands, and out your fingertips. The entire upper half of your body is just a little lighter than the lower half, a little simpler.

Meanwhile, your OCD is getting itchy. It wants to know when you're going to stop this and go back to obsessing! Just nod at the uncomfortable thoughts and feelings. You will return to them soon enough. For now, you're just stepping out for a moment to practice being present.

Breathe into the line and lower it down to your knees. Notice how the remaining tension in your body pools in your shins and calves, as if you're wearing anxiety boots. Finally breathe in, breathe out, and push that line down across your ankles and the tops of your feet, and out your toes.

Finish with another minute or so of just sitting and breathing, always returning to your anchor, the present.

You may feel more relaxed afterward. That's a pleasant side effect of meditation. But more importantly, in terms of changing the way you relate to your OCD, these practices aim to strengthen that muscle in your brain that allows you to disengage from an obsession; accept the uncertainty when the thoughts remain unresolved; and come back, come back, come back to whatever is actually present and real in this moment.

You can do any form of meditation you like, guided or unguided. Start by giving yourself just a minute a day. For many people with OCD, meditation is pretty uncomfortable, because you are being asked to sit with your thoughts and do nothing about them. You are not ignoring them either. You are doing what is, at times, a seemingly impossible task when you have OCD: acknowledging but not responding.

Mindfulness in the Moment

If meditation is doing morning push-ups, then mindfulness practice throughout the day is the equivalent of working in a construction yard. There will be a lot of heavy things to lift throughout the day. Practice disengaging from the OCD urge to judge, analyze, or resolve your thoughts. Return to the present, whatever it may be.

You can help yourself practice mindfulness throughout the day by exchanging whatever OCD rumination may be occurring for attending to something real in the moment. This is not distraction. This is attention. Place things in your life that you value that warrant your attention. When you have a thought, acknowledge it, say hello to it, and then return to whatever exists and is real for you in that moment. Set up hobbies for yourself. Listen to audiobooks in the car. Be social. Do all of these things in moderation, but then moderate your moderation by allowing them to be overdone sometimes.

Sometimes you are willing to let go of an obsession and attend to the present, but there seems to be no obvious attention-demanding activity in front of you. The fact that it's possible to believe this shows how accustomed you have become to having the mind leave the present. You automate life and forget that there are tiny variations in the taste of the food you are eating, unique complexities in the music you listen to, a trillion complex interactions taking place when you are stuck in traffic, and countless physical sensations occurring in your fingertips as you flip through the pages of this book. Use this space to list things that may warrant more attention in the present moment than you give them credit for:

_____

_____

_____

_____

_____

CHAPTER 2

Mindfulness and Cognitive Therapy

While some debate looms about the effectiveness of the emphasis on the *cognitive* part of cognitive behavioral treatment for OCD (Clark 2005), the general consensus is that a significant problem for OCD sufferers is in how they appraise the significance and relevance of the thoughts they are having (Barrera and Norton 2011). In other words, when you become aware of thoughts that trigger you, you make assumptions about the meaning of those thoughts, and this drives you toward compulsions.

Cognitive Therapy

During the 1950s, a therapist by the name of Aaron Beck noticed that people were having strong emotional responses to certain kinds of thoughts that came up in the course of psychoanalysis. This led to an examination of how thoughts lead to emotions, and how emotions influence behavior. Through this process, he developed *cognitive therapy*, which posited that the faulty or distorted interpretation of a person's experience correlated with her dysfunctional behavior (Weinrach 1988). Certain types of thoughts became correlated with certain responses, and when these thought *types* could be identified, the responses could be changed. Beck called these thoughts "hot cognitions" (Bloch 2004). They are also commonly referred to as "automatic thoughts."

Beck took the concept of automatic thoughts and developed a list of what are called *cognitive distortions*. You may also find the term *mistaken*, or *faulty*, *beliefs* used interchangeably with cognitive distortions. Cognitive distortions can best be understood as lenses that we put over our thoughts that affect how we view them. They are the mechanisms by which we are derailed from mindfulness and fall victim to automatic thoughts. A thought happens, and rather than experience the thought simply as it *is*, we push the thought through a lens that distorts it and spits it out as something quite more troubling.

Challenging Cognitive Distortions

Challenging distorted thinking is a delicate process when you are using mindfulness to help relieve your OCD. Challenging the thoughts requires you to pay a level of attention to them that gives them some intrinsic importance. Yet leaving distorted patterns of thinking *un*challenged allows the mind to repeat faulty patterns that lead you to believe that you must act on compulsions.

If you can notice when you are engaging in cognitive distortions, you can identify them as part of the language of OCD. This doesn't mean that you disown or disassociate from them. They are your thoughts, but they don't define who you are. They are spoken in a language based on fear, not on evidence.

By using mindfulness to notice what your mind is doing—calling it out and saying, *I'm doing* _____ (name of distortion)—you are simultaneously accepting it as it is and challenging it. When you become aware that your mind is engaging in a *way* of thinking, you open yourself to the opportunity to release that thinking and return to the present. The power of noticing when your thinking is distorted is the crossroad between cognitive therapy and mindfulness.

When you challenge a distorted way of thinking, it's important to remember that you are challenging the distortion, not the thought itself. In other words, you may have a thought about being dirty. That's the thought you are having, so trying to convince yourself that you are clean will only push you in the direction of washing. However, challenging such notions as, *Because I had a thought about being dirty, I must wash* can give you the freedom to make a noncompulsive choice. So the goal is not to prove your fears away, but to demonstrate to your mind that you can be in the presence of your fear without having to respond to it with compulsions.

The first step in applying mindfulness to cognitive therapy is practicing being aware of when you are engaging in one or more cognitive distortions. In the next several pages, we will look at some of the more commonly understood faulty beliefs found in OCD and discuss strategies for challenging them without doing compulsions. We have combined and modified some beliefs to make them more specific to the OCD process.

All-or-Nothing/Black-and-White/Absolutist/Dichotomous Thinking: Seeing things as being one way or the other, with no in-between

The Problem

This is, by far, the most common distorted lens through which we view our OCD. We live in a world that seems very black and white. Movies have good guys and bad guys; things are either clean or dirty, pure or evil, safe or dangerous, and so on. But this is not the real world. Yes, we may have dark charcoals and bright eggshells, but there's no such thing as black and white. Real life always involves some amount of gray. So if you find yourself thinking, *I am dirty because I touched a public doorknob*, you are allowing OCD to run the show by even suggesting that you were "clean" in the first place. You were probably somewhere in between clean and dirty, and after touching that uncomfortable public item, you were, at best, somewhat dirtier on one hand than you were before.

You may notice that you assume that you are a bad person when you have a thought that you believe is a "bad" thought. Yet somewhere inside you is a rational voice acknowledging that no matter how "bad" the thought is, it can't switch you from one spectrum of morality to another in a second. What are some OCD thoughts that you view as all-or-nothing issues?

_____

_____

The Challenge

If your mind is being too black and white, what would be the gray area? What would be a way of saying the objective truth that accounts for the fact that it's neither 100 percent good nor bad? Usually this involves saying something more diplomatic. For example, if you were anxious during a night out, you might think, *It was difficult to enjoy myself*, instead of, *The evening was ruined*. Another example might be that if you said something that hurt someone's feelings, you might think, *I'm unhappy with the choice I made to say that*, instead of, *I'm a horrible person*. Look at the previous examples you wrote for your all-or-nothing beliefs and see if you can reword them to reflect the more gray reality. Don't worry about getting this right just yet. This is a skill, and like any skill, it's meant to be done poorly before it can be honed. What ideas do you have for challenging your more black-and-white distortions?

_____

_____

_____

Catastrophizing/Predicting/Jumping to Conclusions: Assuming that a feared scenario will play out in the future

The Problem

OCD loves catastrophizing, because it lays out the biggest trap of all, the idea that we can predict the future. We can't predict the future. You may be very bright and really good at guessing, but you are not a psychic. OCD will tell you that if you don't do your compulsions, you will fall apart, someone will get hurt, the world will end, and your worst fears will come true! The thoughts may present themselves in such a way that you are not only thinking about a horrible future, but also predicting your inability to tolerate or cope with that future. What kind of terrifying predictions does your OCD make?

_____

_____

The Challenge

If your automatic thoughts start with _I will_ or some other prediction, then you can always start with an admission of fact: _I can't predict the future._ Now, what could you say if you included this fact? Probably something like, _This thing_ may _happen, but I don't know for sure. If it_ does, _that could be bad, and I might have to come up with a way of dealing with it._ This doesn't mean that your prediction is definitely wrong. Maybe the worst thing you can think of _will_ come to pass. It's okay if that last sentence spiked you a bit. It's hard to accept an idea like that. But in objective reality, you don't know if your fear will come to pass, so behaving as if you _do_ know is just working overtime for the OCD. Rather than trying to convince yourself that your catastrophic fears are guaranteed not to happen, how can you reword your previous catastrophizing examples to reflect an acknowledgment that the future is unknown, or that you lack evidence for your prediction?

_____

Magnifying: Taking something as it is and making it bigger

The Problem

If you have health anxiety, your freckles seem like moles, and your moles seem like cancerous tumors. If you find yourself aware of "bad" thoughts, you think they are the worst thoughts anyone has ever had. Every cold seems like a horrible disease, every raised voice seems like an act of violence, and every error in judgment seems like a federal crime. What are some thoughts that run through your head that seem horrendous but, in moments of calm clarity, seem like just, well, stuff?

The Challenge

If you're "making a mountain out of a molehill," try to just acknowledge that it's a molehill. That doesn't mean it's safe. It just means acknowledging what something is *as it is*. If your OCD says, *That red mark on my shoe is disease-infected blood*, you could simply acknowledge that what you actually know is *There is a red mark on my shoe, and I'm uncomfortable*. Again, you're not trying to disprove the OCD. You're just making the case that it doesn't deserve the attention it's getting. How could you describe in a more observational way the magnifications in the previous examples you wrote?

Discounting or Disqualifying the Positive: Purposely shutting down or blocking out evidence that your fears are OCD related

The Problem

In cognitive science, the term *confirmation bias* describes the common human mistake of interpreting evidence in a manner that supports our preexisting beliefs (Nickerson 1998).

The main way in which we fall into this trap is by discounting evidence that opposes our beliefs. When you've been triggered, your entire life experience seems to go out the window, and the only thing you keep hearing is that your fears are true. You may be the most devoted father on earth, but the moment you had a thought about shaking your crying baby, you started sentencing yourself to death for a lifetime of being an abusive father. When your OCD is telling you that noticing the beautiful actress on TV means you're unfaithful, you might forget that you've had multiple opportunities to cheat on your spouse, none of which you have chosen to act on. You may also find it practically impossible to take a compliment due to your commitment to shutting down compliments, only because they run contrary to what you hear in your head all day. Taking yes for an answer and accepting that the evidence in front of you supports that you are *probably* okay may elude you in an OCD episode. When do you sometimes disregard evidence that runs contrary to your obsessions?

_____

_____

The Challenge

Although an experience doesn't necessarily prove anything, you can use it to challenge an assumption. So if you are struggling with sexual orientation OCD, you may be discounting your life experience of being with one kind of person. You can challenge this by responding, *In my experience, I have typically chosen to be with this kind of person.* Notice how we are intentionally resisting addressing the orientation itself. We are simply stating that the claim of the OCD thoughts isn't supported by historical evidence. What are some ways you can challenge your disqualifying distortions?

_____

_____

_____

Emotional Reasoning: Using feelings as evidence of the veracity of your fears

The Problem

As discussed in chapter 1, feelings aren't facts. Of course, we use our emotions to make sense of reality. It's just that OCD has its thumb firmly placed on the "fear" button. So we find ourselves thinking that something must be true because it just feels that way! Your upcoming performance feels as if it will be a disaster because you are nervous. You may think you will be violently attacked because you feel unsafe. Challenging emotional reasoning requires separating the experience of *having a feeling* from the *meaning* that the feeling may imply. Feeling at risk doesn't place you at risk. Feeling ashamed doesn't make you a person of low worth. What are ways in which you notice yourself thinking that things are true only because they *feel* that way?

The Challenge

You can challenge thoughts that something bad will happen or has happened because it *feels* that way by simply stating that what you feel and what you *do* don't line up 100 percent of the time. The mindfulness element here is that you are acknowledging that the feelings you are having are simply the feelings you are having. OCD insists that these feelings must *mean* some specific thing. You are challenging OCD's *logic*, not whether it's right or wrong. For example, a statement of emotional reasoning for someone with violent obsessions might be, *I'm going to hurt someone, because I feel angry and freaked out.* A challenging statement might be something like, *I feel angry in this moment and don't know what's going to happen, but typically my being angry doesn't result in people getting harmed.* Someone with contamination OCD might think, *I have to wash because I feel dirty*, which can be challenged with, *Feeling dirty doesn't show me the dirt.* How can you challenge some of your mistaken assumptions about feelings as facts?

Selective Abstraction/Zeroing In/Tunnel Vision: Focusing exclusively or excessively on things that relate to your fear

The Problem

Although it may appear as such, everything is *not* always about your OCD. *Selective abstraction* works by making you tie every experience you have into whatever you are obsessed with. It's as if you were wearing red-tinted glasses, looking up at a clear, blue sky, and swearing that it was purple. Yes, it may look that way, but still you understand that the sky is not purple. It's as if the things that relate to your obsession are somehow more visible, further out in front. It's a similar phenomenon to hearing a lot of love songs on the radio after breaking up with someone. The love songs were there before, but you are selectively abstracting them *from* your environment and connecting them to your thoughts. What does it sound like in your mind when you are only noticing the obsession instead of the bigger picture?

_____

_____

The Challenge

If you notice that the problem with what your mind is doing is that you are singling out some negative detail related to your obsession and missing the bigger picture, then take the opportunity to look at the bigger picture. This is a true mindfulness challenge in which you can acknowledge your mind pattern: that you tend to associate things with your obsession. The association doesn't mean that these things are actually linked anywhere but in your mind. Here you can take the opportunity to respond, *I tend to notice these things because of my OCD, but it's not necessary to pay extra attention to them just because they relate to my obsession.* Using your own language, how can you challenge your mind when it's zeroing in on something related to an obsession?

_____

_____

_____

"Should" Statements/Perfectionism/Overcontrol: Applying a rigid set of rules about your obsession that can never be bent or modified

The Problem

People without OCD sometimes say things like, "I'm so OCD about that," and it may feel insensitive to you because of how much pain your perfectionism has caused you. It's not that your standards are too high. It's that the standards *rise* the closer you get to achieving them! In reality, perfection is the perpetual state in which something horrible is about to happen. Anything that changes what's perfect automatically destroys it. So perfection is an illusion, not something that we actually want, because it's not something that actually exists. Still, the OCD throws the words "should" and "must" into the equation, and we feel helpless against compulsive responses. You may tell yourself that you *should always* be health conscious, even though you want to have a doughnut for breakfast on a lazy Sunday morning. If you have obsessions of a sexual or violent nature, you may berate yourself for having the thoughts, believing that you *must never* think them. You may feel that you *should* be able to recall the details of *every* conversation and *must* comprehend *every* word of *every* book you read. It's exhausting. The real problem with making "should" statements and trying to overcontrol your thoughts is that the practice mutually excludes accepting what *is*, and thus, it is the destroyer of mindfulness. If something should be one way and happens not to be that way, that means it cannot be accepted the way it is. That leaves no room for mindfulness. What are some rigid rules that you impose about your OCD fears?

The Challenge

If your OCD says you *must* never have this thought or you *should* do this or that compulsion, you can challenge this by addressing the rigidity of the statement. Take the opportunity to throw mindfulness at the OCD: *I notice that I have an urge to do my compulsion, but there's no such thing as "should" or "must." I can choose and be flexible in my choices.* If, for example, you struggle with a compulsive urge for symmetry, you might be thinking, *I must line up those books the right way.* You can challenge this with, *I have an urge to line up those books and could challenge my OCD by letting them be.* Sometimes it can be helpful to replace "should" with the expression, *It would benefit me to...* See if your "should" statement still makes sense after that. Other than reducing your temporary anxiety, would it *benefit* you to drive back home to check whether the stove was turned off? Other than compulsively quieting the OCD beast in the short term, would it *benefit* you to stay several hours late at work, redoing a project to make certain it was perfect? What are some ideas for challenging your more perfectionist beliefs?

Comparing and Contrasting: Looking at the experience of another person and using it to frame your own experience negatively

The Problem

Generally, we can't control the fact that we are social creatures who compare and contrast ourselves to others. The comparing and contrasting are not the problem. The problem is our assuming that the comparisons we are making are particularly interesting or important and that we need to *do* something about them. You might compare yourself to the non-OCD population and think they have it easy, but the truth is they have their own problems. And you may compare your body to that of a supermodel, your intellect to that of someone you think is a genius, or your religious faith to that of your spiritual advisor, but ultimately, comparing provides only distorted information. Whoever you are comparing yourself to has different genetics, had a different childhood, went to a different school, has held different jobs, and so on. Even your siblings had different experiences than you did in your family, in part because they grew up with you in their lives. So this other person to whom you compare yourself is really just that: *another person*. The OCD may make it seem as if that person were just a version of you that somehow made better choices. But how is this possible? You may not have made all the best choices in life, but that's not what you thought at the time you were making them. What qualities do you think other people have that you're supposed to have?

The Challenge

Challenging distortions begins with acknowledging that the comparing is a behavior, something you are *doing*, something that can be rejected or let go of, once recognized. So if the thought is *My coworker is smarter than I am*, the challenge could be *I don't need to compare myself to other people and don't know all of the assets and defects of my coworker anyway*. Another viable challenge to comparison thoughts is mindfully stating the obvious. For example, *That person doesn't have to deal with stupid obsessions* can be challenged with *Other people are other people. I don't know what they deal with*. What are some ways you can challenge the comparisons you make?

Mind Reading and Personalizing: Theorizing about the thoughts of other people or attributing their behavior to your obsession

The Problem

You might believe that you know what people are thinking or why they do the things they do, especially if you consider yourself to be "intuitive." But just as with catastrophizing, all this means is that you are good at guessing. You don't *know* what other people think or why they make the choices they make. It's not possible. Even if they *tell* you, you can't prove that they're being honest. So whenever thoughts show up that start with *They think…*, you can pretty much assume that the OCD is tricking you. A good example of personalizing would be if someone abruptly exited a conversation. You might think that the definite reason this happened was that you said something to offend the other person. The truth is, she may have had a stomach bug, or been embarrassed by her own intrusive thoughts! If you struggle with sexual obsessions, you might presume that someone smiled at you because he wanted to let you know that he thought you were attracted to him. If you have harm OCD, you might think that someone who's putting the dishes away is trying to keep you from being around knives. What does it sound like in your mind when your fears of what other people are thinking or doing push you to do compulsions?

_____

_____

The Challenge

If your mind is busying itself with thoughts of what others are thinking or why others are doing things, then you can always challenge it with, *I can't read minds, and I don't know why people do things.* From there you can ask yourself if your theory about what someone *may* be thinking is sufficient evidence to prompt you to seek reassurance, or if this is just more OCD trickery. If you are personalizing someone's behavior, you can acknowledge, *Maybe that person said that because of my obsession, and maybe they didn't. I don't have to do anything about it right now.* Using your own words, what are some ways you can challenge your mind-reading and personalizing assumptions?

_____

_____

_____

Hyperresponsibility: Thinking that you alone are to be held accountable for preventing tragic events

The Problem

OCD can use all kinds of exaggerations and twisted logic to get you to thinking that you're the only one who could possibly keep something horrible from happening and that if you have shirked this responsibility, you are truly evil incarnate. Someone falling victim to hyperresponsibility obsessions may find herself decontaminating things excessively for the benefit of the next person who may encounter something she used. You may feel the need to move something like a coin or gum wrapper from the middle of the street, because OCD says that a driver might get distracted and that the resulting accident would be your fault! In his powerful memoir on OCD, *Rewind, Replay, Repeat*, author Jeff Bell (2007) describes the painful lengths he went through to be certain that a traffic cone left by a construction crew wouldn't cause an accident. When do you notice that you are holding yourself to an impossible standard of responsibility that drives you to act on compulsions?

_____

_____

The Challenge

Your OCD may be saying that you have to check the coffeemaker at work even though someone else already did this, because if *you* don't, something horrible will happen. The OCD is saying that it's important for you to be good, not irresponsible and selfish. This can be challenged with something like, *Compulsively checking for the purpose of avoiding guilt isn't the same thing as being a good person. I'll have to take the risk and accept that I can't be responsible for everything all the time.* You can challenge the philosophy behind the idea that you must be responsible 100 percent of the time. You can also acknowledge that there are many potential consequences to your failure to act on the hyperresponsibility thought and that you don't know for certain that they are all bad. What are some challenges to your mind's tendency to be overly responsible?

_____

_____

_____

Magical or Superstitious Thinking/Thought-Action Fusion: Subscribing to the idea that thinking something makes it more likely to become an action or event, or that merely having the thought is the same as an event occurring

The Problem

Magical thinking plays a significant role in the mental constructs of people with OCD, especially in regards to checking compulsions (Einstein and Menzies 2004). Several times already, while going through this workbook, you probably have been asked to write things that made you feel very uncomfortable. You may have thought that writing them, and thus *thinking them on purpose*, would make them more likely to come true. How? Magic. You may have read some disturbing things written in this book and fear that now that you have seen these words, they are there just for you and that now they are more likely to result in something terrible happening. How? Magic. Magical thinking can trick your mind into believing things you would otherwise think are ridiculous. It does this by suggesting that your being wrong isn't worth the risk, that if your thoughts *did* have magical properties, you wouldn't be able to tolerate finding out the hard way. Fusing your thoughts with actions fundamentally attributes an importance to thoughts that they don't have, thus compromising your ability to practice mindfulness. Thought-action fusion can be experienced as an issue of morality (as in thinking something bad equals *doing* something bad) or an issue of likelihood (as in thinking that something will happen means it's more likely to happen) (Berman et al. 2011). What are some areas in your experience of OCD where you feel that the presence of a thought is the equivalent to an action or could bring about an event?

_____

_____

The Challenge

Thought-action fusion can be tricky to challenge if you find yourself really stuck to the belief that thoughts *in* your head can cause events to occur *outside* your head. For most people, these types of distortions are easily challenged with, *Magic is silly, and I don't have to be certain about these things.* But even if the fusion of thoughts and actions in your head seems unbreakable, you can still challenge the rigidity: *I don't know for certain that my thoughts will cause these bad things to happen. No compulsion will give me this certainty, so I'll have to take the risk if I want to get better.* This is a good opportunity to assess the OCD thought for evidence while treading carefully to resist too much analysis. For example, the thought, *My wife will get in a car accident, because I thought about a crash and didn't tell myself she's going to be okay*, can be challenged with, *I don't have any evidence that my thoughts can cause car accidents*. What are some ways in which you can challenge the magical thinking that your mind engages in?

_____

_____

_____

Automatic Thought Records

One of the primary tools used in cognitive therapy (Bennett-Levy 2003), the *automatic thought record* is used for practicing the types of challenges you worked on previously. The way the thought record works for OCD is that you document situations that trigger you, identify the automatic thoughts the mind is picking up from the OCD, and shift them toward a more objective (and essentially more mindful) stance.

Traditional thought records often include additional columns for other helpful information, such as rating your feelings, and the results of your behavioral choice. We prefer to use a simplified version that includes only the trigger, the automatic thought, and the challenge. To use mindfulness alongside cognitive therapy as a weapon against OCD, it's important to assess the distorted thinking quickly and simply. Otherwise you may get stuck reviewing your thoughts, adding value to them, and engaging in mental rituals that render mindfulness obsolete.

By practicing challenging your distorted thoughts in this way, you give your mind a place to go other than where the OCD demands that it goes. For example, if you are triggered by having touched something you think is dirty, you are likely to have an automatic thought about being contaminated and having to wash. If you record this event in a thought record and write down your challenge to the distorted thought (for example, *I don't know if my hands are dirty, and I can tolerate feeling uncomfortable*), you are presenting another place to which your mind can go. The next time you get triggered, you may have the same automatic thought, but that, in and of itself, will remind you of the alternatives that you had practiced writing down. Rather than your having to dig for them, more rational, non-OCD thoughts will begin to present themselves.

The most important thing to remember about using the automatic thought record as a cognitive therapy tool is that the goal is not reassurance. The goal is to not do compulsions and to embrace mindful acceptance of the triggering situation.

Automatic Thought Record

Trigger What set you off?	Automatic Thought What is the OCD saying?	Challenge What is an alternative to the distorted thinking?

CHAPTER 3

Mindfulness and Behavioral Therapy

You have likely heard of Pavlov and his famous experiment in which he repeatedly offered food to a dog while ringing a bell. While dogs instinctually salivate in the presence of food, Pavlov's dog eventually came to salivate just from the sound of a bell, even when no food was present. This *learned response* is a result of a process known as *Pavlovian conditioning* or *classical conditioning* (Clark 2004). Through this process, the dog's salivation response became *bound* to the stimulus (the sound of the bell). Likewise, in OCD, the feeling state of anxiety becomes *bound* to our unwanted thoughts. Just as dogs don't instinctually salivate in response to the sound of a bell, people don't naturally have an instinctual response of anxiety to their thoughts. The person with OCD involuntarily *learns* over time (via classical conditioning) to have an anxiety response in reaction to thoughts that most other people perceive as benign.

The concept of conditioning was further developed by psychologist B. F. Skinner, whose research demonstrated that we modify our behavior in response to rewards and consequences, a process he called *operant conditioning* (Staddon and Cerutti 2003). People with OCD act on compulsions in order to relieve their distress. But by relieving our distress, our compulsions actually lead to more compulsions, for the simple reason that we are naturally more likely to repeat any behavior that results in a reduction of discomfort. This is called *negative reinforcement*, because it involves the removal of a negative experience, such as anxiety.

So while compulsive behaviors temporarily remove the negative experience of anxiety and discomfort, the OCD traps you in a loop of negative reinforcement. Your triggering thought results in distress, which leads you to act compulsively in an effort to relieve that distress, which provides temporary relief but actually "reinforces" the compulsive behavior, thus leading you to do more compulsions the next time your anxiety reappears. This loop is called the *obsessive-compulsive cycle*:

The Obsessive-Compulsive Cycle

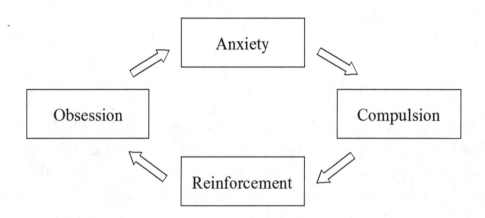

When we choose to change our behavioral reaction to an unwanted thought, we may at first feel very uncomfortable. But eventually our minds adapt to this new pairing through a process called *habituation*. By stopping our compulsive and avoidant behaviors, we stop the negative reinforcement and learn over time that we *can* tolerate the presence of our unwanted thoughts. The end result is that thoughts that were once a *trigger* are no longer so triggering.

In the world of behavioral psychotherapy, the commonly accepted viewpoint on the relationship between the brain, the mind, and the self is that you cannot control what thoughts, feelings, and physical sensations you have. Your job is to choose your behaviors. When you have OCD, you may find yourself presented with internal data that seems absurd, horrific, or threatening. The presence or lack thereof of this information isn't something you can control. When you control your *behavior*, you teach the mind how to frame the experience.

You Don't Decide What Happens Inside

You are not your brain. Your brain is a bodily organ, and one of the things it does is generate thoughts. You may be able to dig up thoughts, and this may make you varying degrees of clever, but you didn't generate the thoughts. You *collected* them from the soup in your brain. You have no say in what kinds of thoughts happen to occur and what kinds of thoughts your mind's radar happens to pick up. If you are trying to control your thoughts, by judging them or attempting to suppress them, then you are doing a compulsion. You only get to decide what you *do* with your thoughts, not what thoughts you happen to have.

The same is true of feelings. Sometimes you feel happy, and it's not because anything in particular is going your way. You just feel happy. Sometimes you feel fear that's not necessarily connected to anything important either. Can we better stabilize and regulate our emotions? Sure. Can we keep our emotions from determining our behavior? Absolutely. But if all it took was simply controlling what feelings we had, we'd all be happy all the time.

Physical sensations, urges, impulses—these little bits of data we get from the body—also come and go as they please. Their relevance to your life is grounded completely in how you respond to them. Responding to them with distorted thinking or with compulsive behaviors simply highlights their presence in your life.

All we have complete control over is our behavior. This is true 100 percent of the time. This is hard to accept at first when you suffer from OCD. Most of the time, you find yourself doing things precisely because you believe you absolutely have to in order to survive. But ultimately compulsions are behavioral choices—very difficult, painful choices.

Change the Behavior, and the Thoughts and Feelings Follow

If you have a thought about spiders being deadly and with it comes a feeling of being in danger, a logical rational behavior would be to avoid spiders at all costs. If there's no reason to ever be around spiders or anything that reminds you of them, this avoidant behavior will work just fine with your thoughts and feelings. But if you have some reason to get rid of your thoughts and feelings about spiders, you won't see much change without a change in your behavior taking the lead. Maybe you have fallen in love with someone who has a pet spider. You want to be around your sweetie, but that means being around spiders—and *that* means thinking you're going to die a horrible death. So you might go to a therapist and ask to have your thoughts and feelings removed. That doesn't work.

A good CBT therapist will show you how to *move the behavior* so that the thoughts and feelings naturally gravitate in that direction. What this means is that you would have to engage in a plan of behaving as if spiders were tolerable *before* you could expect thoughts that they will kill you and feelings of danger to lighten up. It might start with something simple, like looking at pictures of spiders. At first look, thoughts and feelings might convey the message, *This is too much!* But over time, through habituation, thoughts and feelings will begin to communicate, *Pictures of spiders are no big deal.*

In the beginning, it's a terrible feeling indeed to have your behavior on one end of reality and your thoughts and feelings on another. Typically, the thoughts are the first to join the behavior, and this is where behavioral therapy is the most challenging. Here you are behaving as if spiders aren't so terrible by not avoiding them, and at the same time, you're thinking, *Well, I'm not a fan of spiders, but I probably won't die a horrible death today.* But your *feelings*, stubborn as they are, still haven't caught up. They're still telling you that you're in danger. They're begging you to come back to avoidance. Using mindfulness, you dig in and commit to the behavior, independently from the feelings, and you stay with that behavior until your feelings get the idea. And some time may pass before the physical sensations, such as increased heart rate, start to shift as well. But eventually you work up to higher and higher behavioral expressions of acceptance, and guide the thoughts and feelings wherever you believe they are best suited. This is known as "graduated exposure with response prevention," and it's an essential part of OCD treatment.

Exposure with Response Prevention

Exposure with response prevention (ERP) involves "systematic, repeated, and prolonged exposure to situations that provoke obsessional fear, along with abstinence from compulsive behaviors" (Abramowitz 2006). In short, you purposely get in front of your fears, either in literal, physical terms (for example, touching something that upsets you) or in theoretical terms (for example, imagining a feared situation), and you practice resisting the compulsive response.

ERP is about demonstrating for your mind what it needs to better process the false information about the things you fear. If you want to stop obsessing about something, you have to stop responding to thoughts and feelings about that thing as if they were important. But to do that takes practice. You have to *expose* yourself to the things you are afraid of (which may be actual things or just thoughts and feelings), and you have to *prevent* yourself from the automatic *response*, which would be the compulsion to neutralize, suppress, or otherwise undo whatever your brain is presenting to you.

In Vivo Exposure

Mindfulness is exposure. It's exposure to what happens when you experience a thought, accept its presence as a thought, and then don't do compulsions. It's exposure to what happens when you let a terrifying thought go, as if it didn't matter that it was terrifying, without insisting on ascertaining the meaning of that thought. It's exposure to feeling terrified and not allowing this to determine your behavior. Perhaps your constant battle with a particular idea—whether it's contamination, harm, relationships, sexual orientation, or anything else—is consuming your every waking moment. You need to change the role that this obsession plays in your life.

Exposure means that you are opening up to something, as a camera lens exposes to light. Response prevention means that you are stopping something from happening in connection with your exposure. In simple terms, what you are trying to accomplish by doing ERP is getting some time in the ring with your fears instead of constantly running.

Your mind has learned that obsessions must be followed by compulsions. It has calculated this carefully based on your observed behavior. If you can demonstrate to your mind that you are capable of being in front of your fears *without* doing compulsions, then your mind has to admit that compulsions are a *choice*. If that's true, it must mean that the obsessions are not as automatically important as previously assumed. If *that's* true, then they may not be worth any response, let alone a compulsive one.

You may have seen some portrayals of ERP in the media in which people were forced to do disgusting things, dangerous things, and ridiculous things all at once. This is not ERP. While exposure definitely involves pushing your limits, it's not about learning to swim by being shoved into the deep end of the pool while your therapist yells at you to swim. We're building brain muscles here. If we were building body muscles, we wouldn't start with a two-hundred-pound barbell. You'll put your back out and stop coming to the gym. We also don't waste too much time with empty gestures in ERP. You may lift a two-pound dumbbell at the gym, but don't delude yourself into thinking that this will give you bulging biceps. What you want is to start somewhere challenging but achievable, and you want to do this thing until it's no longer too challenging—and then you raise the weights.

The Compulsive Hierarchy

The first step to doing ERP is to know what you're up against. You will need a list of things to do exposure with and responses to be prevented if you are going to do ERP. You can look up your specific obsession in part 2 of this workbook to get some examples of the kinds of things people sometimes include in this list. Don't worry about the order you put them in; we'll do that next. After reading the following items, use the space that comes after them to write your list:

1. List any compulsion that you do. This includes any physical or mental ritual that you engage in to make yourself feel okay when you're faced with an obsession. Also include any routine behavior that you do excessively because of OCD and any ways in which you seek reassurance related to your obsessions (for example, asking others about your obsessions, confessing your thoughts, visiting websites related to your obsessions, and so on).

2. List anything that you avoid because of your obsession. You may avoid some things consciously because you are often near them (for example, knives, cats, cars). You may rarely avoid some things because you seldom see them, but the idea of seeing them triggers a strong urge to avoid (for example, pornography involving a different sexual orientation from your own, horror movies, and so on).

_____

_____

_____

_____

_____

_____

_____

_____

_____

_____

_____

_____

_____

Now take a look at each item on your list and consider what it would be like to be in front of your trigger without doing that compulsion. How hard would it be? How much discomfort would you feel? You can give it a numeric value if that helps. Don't worry about accuracy. You are likely to change your mind about the difficulty level and move it up or down many times during your ERP experience. Now, in the following space, rewrite your list in order of easiest to approach to hardest to approach:

_____

_____

_____

_____

_____

_____

_____

_____

_____

_____

_____

_____

_____

_____

_____

This is what you are up against. These are the things you need to remove from your life to overcome your obsessions. You will knock each of them out one at a time. You will use the power of your mind to demonstrate to your OCD brain that you are not a slave to your thoughts.

Generally, you want to keep in mind that the things you are exposing yourself to, whether they are images or physical items, are just _things_. You may not be as afraid of these things as you believe. What's more likely is that you are afraid of how bad you _feel_ when you are around these things. To do exposure effectively, it needs to generate that feeling that you are so invested in avoiding. You need to participate in generating this feeling. If you didn't feel such pain in the presence of a trigger, you wouldn't consider it important to avoid that trigger.

The goal is not to enjoy the thing you are exposing to, although in some cases, you may become an aficionado of things that previously frightened you (such as scary movies or guns). The goal is actually mindfulness itself. It's freedom from the automatic reaction. It's creating a space that allows the mind to view the trigger as a _thing_. Through repetition, all things return to their natural place in the universe. Today the doorknob to a public restroom may appear to be a radioactive, festering _E. coli_ factory. But through repeated contact, it eventually becomes a doorknob again. What may be on the doorknob remains uncertain, but your increased tolerance of uncertainty allows for that. So what you are trying to win back through ERP is the ability to be mindful, to see things as they actually *are* instead of only what you fear they could be.

Now that you have a basic hierarchy, you will want to translate each compulsion into an exposure assignment or a series of exposure assignments. Start with the first one on your list. Perhaps you compulsively wash your hands five times after using the bathroom. There are a number of things you could do to confront the fear of what would happen if you resisted this compulsion. You could change the number of washings from five to four. You could reduce the amount of soap, the duration of each washing, and the frequency.

If your compulsion is to avoid being triggered by violent imagery, think of things with violent imagery that you can handle. It could be watching the local news or watching a trailer for a horror film. Take a moment to make some notes next to each of your entries with ideas for exposures. Don't worry if they don't make much sense. You may never do any of them, or you may do all of them. You may do one and find that it was harder than you anticipated, and then go back to working on something easier. You are in control of your behavior, and you are in control of your treatment.

Right now you are just opening up a window to let some light in so that you can see what relieving your OCD would actually involve. If this task seems a bit daunting right now, skip it until you've read more about your obsession in part 2 of this book, and then come back. Use the following space to write ideas for doing direct exposure with your triggers. What would generate the urge to act on compulsions so that you can practice resisting them?

_____

_____

_____

_____

_____

_____

_____

_____

_____

_____

_____

Imaginal Exposure

You may be thinking, *What if my fear is about doing something unacceptable to me or to society? I can't do exposure with something that hurts someone or permanently changes who I am!*

To do ERP for *ideas*, we need to be more creative. Here's where mindfulness plays a key role in OCD. To do exposure in the mind, we must create maps to guide us to the fear. We then follow those maps through a process called *imaginal exposure*. Another term for imaginal exposure that you may hear is *scripting*. It's called this because you write a story, or a script, in which you describe your OCD fear as if it were coming true. In an imaginal exposure script, you are writing that which will generate your discomfort. You are practicing inviting the worst of the worst instead of running from it. With each statement, you are trying to raise your discomfort level and hold it there.

At the core of mindfulness is acknowledging that these are the thoughts going through your head. Rather than have you compulsively deny or avoid these thoughts that are going through your head, an imaginal exposure script blasts them from a megaphone. If you consider your unwanted thoughts to be like a train passing through your head, imaginal scripting is a way to pull it through. Compulsions are futile strategies for stopping the train, something that only results in more pain.

An imaginal script typically starts with a basic admission that you have done something wrong, that you are currently the embodiment of something unacceptable to you, or that you will engage in some future behavior that's intolerable.

Here are some generic examples:

I will think about this obsession forever.

I'm this kind of person.

I will engage in an unacceptable act.

I did a terrible thing.

See if you can use your mind in this moment to distill what you are afraid of and say that it's true. Whatever crime you are compulsively trying to convince yourself isn't real, go ahead and write it down here. Don't be surprised if this brief activity is extremely triggering, and don't beat yourself up if you feel unready to put these words to paper. Let yourself be aware that right now, this is an exposure, and try to allow yourself to feel whatever it elicits in you.

_____

_____

_____

_____

_____

If you were up to the challenge, then you've just written one of the worst things you could find at the far outskirts of your mind. You might feel your OCD ramping up a bit with urges to analyze and process what you wrote. Usually when your OCD begins to talk, you jump in and shut it up with a compulsion. Here you will let it talk and talk and talk (this is the exposure), and you will resist reassurance and avoidance (this is the response prevention). So let's use the mind to travel to the next scary stop on the mental landscape. What will you have to do next, now that your fear is a reality?

Now that I've admitted this, I will have to…

_____

_____

_____

_____

You may be feeling pretty uncomfortable right now. We're not going to invest too heavily in a full-on exposure script right now, because you'll be guided through that in part 2 for your specific obsession. Right now we're just looking at the blueprints of the skill you'll need to develop. So try not to take it too seriously just yet. If you need a break, take one and then come back. If you're ready to move on, let's consider that you've just written about engaging in some unacceptable behavior. What happens next?

_____

_____

_____

How are you affected by the knowledge that you have acted on your fears?

_____

_____

How are others affected by it? What will they do now that your fear has been realized?

_____

_____

How do you respond to their reaction?

_____

_____

What kind of person does this make you?

_____

_____

How will you be punished for what you've done? Literally? Spiritually? Emotionally?

_____

_____

At what point are you incapable of taking it anymore?

_____

_____

Then what happens?

_____

_____

When you attempt imaginal scripting, you have to be willing to let the OCD annihilate you. It's learning how to take a punch, basically. It's a different kind of fighting the OCD. It's not trading punches. It's getting in the ring and letting the OCD pummel you over and over again. But eventually, the OCD runs out of energy, and although you may be in pain, you never actually fall down. Pema Chödrön (1991, 105) describes a teacher's metaphor of being knocked down by waves and repeatedly standing up again, despite the appearance of a new wave each time: "The waves just keep coming, but each time you get knocked down, you stand up and keep walking. After a while you'll find that the waves appear to be getting smaller." It's the OCD that finally falls from exhaustion. You may be sore and mentally bloodied, but you are the one that remains standing in the end. This is because of the reality behind mindfulness: thoughts cannot kill you.

As with any exposure, you have to repeat it for learning to take place. There are two ways to repeat imaginal exposure. One is to rewrite the story from scratch every day. Devote twenty to thirty minutes every day to entering that scary space in your mind and obsessing as hard as you can without doing compulsions. The story may change each day as you come up with new ways to generate that feeling of fear, but the script still follows the basic format described. Try to remember that the goal is to get that feeling going. That feeling is what you are avoiding as much as the individual thoughts. That feeling is what you need to learn to stop overresponding to.

Another strategy is to write one strong script and reread it several times in a row until you habituate to the discomfort. Or you may record your script in an audio format and play that recording back multiple times each day. The only danger with these approaches to imaginal scripting is that you may have a tendency to "zone out" when you reread or relisten to your script. This can be counterproductive. For scripting to work, you must obsess but, paradoxically, stay mindfully present with the material. That is what generates the discomfort for exposure. If you mentally wander off, you won't see the same results.

Acceptance Scripts

If you were ready to go into the mental state the exposure brought on, you may have gone pretty deep into your OCD experience in the previous activity. If you want to ease into scripting or if you feel you might benefit from extra motivation for resisting compulsions, you can use an *acceptance script*. This script is more like a daily affirmation, but without the compulsive reassurance that everything will be fine. In short, it's a statement of what you will have to *accept* in order to beat your OCD. Whereas many exposure scripts start with, "I don't have OCD. I really have this much scarier issue!" an acceptance script starts with the most important element of mindfulness for OCD:

I have OCD. Because I have OCD, I have to accept that I deal with obsessions and compulsions.

My main obsessions are (list your primary obsessions in short form):

_____

I respond to these obsessions with compulsions. My main compulsions are (list a few of your major compulsions here):

_____

I have to accept that I may never get certainty regarding my obsessions. The only thing I can be certain of is that if I continue to do compulsions, I will continue to be a slave to my OCD.

Now, consider some of the things that you would like to do that your OCD keeps you from doing. This could be anything from using a public restroom to having a relationship.

I deserve to be able to:

_____

_____

_____

_____

I will have to accept unwanted thoughts and feelings when I start to do these things. I won't let my OCD bully me anymore. It may be a long, bumpy road ahead, but I am a person of value and I deserve a fair shot at happiness.

While the acceptance script contains an element of behavioral exposure because you are confronting your fear of uncertainty regarding your obsession, it's meant primarily to orient you toward a mindful, noncompulsive stance. You can read it once or twice a day as something simple that points you in the right direction.

General Exposures

General exposures are not used as individual exercises but as constant reminders. The purpose behind a general exposure is to condition yourself to stop being surprised and impressed whenever a trigger comes up. This creates an environment of no escape, making it impossible to act on compulsions that feel effective.

A good way of doing a general exposure might be to put a picture on the desktop of your computer that reminds you of your obsession. You can also take sayings, words, numbers, and so forth, and place them on sticky notes throughout your home. Take them down when you have guests if you're concerned about it, and then put them back up when your guests leave.

Wear clothes that remind you of your obsession. Drive through specific areas on the way to work that remind you of your obsession. Make your obsession something that cannot be avoided. Through this, you can begin to break down your resistance to the presence of the thoughts and move toward mindful acceptance.

You will, of course, find these reminders upsetting at first, but they will stop bothering you in time. You'll get triggered and feel an urge to do compulsions, but then give up because you'll just get triggered again later by some other reminder. Once you get used to not responding, the general exposures stop being so threatening.

Flooding in the Moment

Another ERP technique is to take the content of your thoughts, the experience of your feelings, and the intensity of your physical sensations and exaggerate them. *Flooding a thought* means taking that thought's contents and purposefully magnifying them. This can come in the form of agreeing with the statement behind the thought, adding more aggressive language to the thought, or trying to increase the discomfort of your anxiety as a direct response to being triggered.

In an ERP exercise, it's important that you not use flooding as a way of checking your reaction, but only as a way of exposing yourself to your fear (we'll examine compulsive flooding in chapter 4). You can use flooding at two levels of intensity. Level one is sarcastic flooding. It means internally responding to the OCD with a *Yeah right, whatever you say.* It's internally shrugging and rolling your eyes: *Oh yeah, ninjas are going to break into my home and kill my family because I left the door unlocked! Ninjas!*

Along these lines, an activity called "Headlines" can bring humor to an otherwise uncomfortable OCD experience. In this activity, you take the feared thought and try to reword it as a newspaper headline. For example, here's a headline version of an obsessive thought about being contaminated by radiation:

"Area Man Grows Third Arm Out of His Back After Unnecessarily Exposing Himself to X-Ray Machine: Could Have Probably Taken a Different Approach and Avoided Embarrassing His Family"

The subheading really seals the deal. Give this activity a shot here. Take an uncomfortable OCD thought and flood it into a "headline":

_____

_____

_____

_____

You can use more-intense flooding as a short, internal-monologue version of an imaginal script. The thought may start with something like, *What if that speed bump I just ran over was actually a body?* The flooding exercise would be to respond with, *It was a homeless man, and I just ran him over. He's dying, bleeding in the street, and I'm going to wake up tomorrow with the police at my doorstep, here to arrest me for fleeing the scene of a crime.* If you feel that you can go there in this moment, try to write a short flooding script below for your obsessive thought. Remember to resist the urge to analyze or neutralize how it makes you feel; instead intentionally raise the intensity of your discomfort.

_____

_____

_____

_____

In the past few chapters, we've looked at different ways to tackle the problem of responding to the OCD experience with compulsions and how to address them with mindfulness and cognitive and behavioral techniques. Next we'll look at the different types of compulsions that exist and the intricacies of identifying and resisting each of them.

CHAPTER 4

Mindfulness and Compulsions

Resisting a compulsion is always an act of mindfulness. It's a choice to respond to your mind by telling it that you have received its message, but that the message wasn't a mandate to act. However, by their very nature, compulsions are difficult to resist. They offer immediate, short-term relief from significant pain, and the very fact that they pay off what you expect from them only a portion of the time makes them that much more addictive! It's like a slot machine where you keep pulling and pulling, and every once in a while, you get that "ding-ding-ding" and some coins fall out. But then immediately afterward, you end up putting those coins right back into the machine!

Common Compulsions

Learning to master your OCD means learning to identify and resist compulsions. Identifying compulsions means looking at what you are doing in response to the OCD. *Looking* at what you are doing is an act of mindfulness.

Although some compulsions are overt physical acts, others may be covert mental rituals. There's also a gray area to consider. For example, reassurance seeking can be a physical ritual if you are verbally asking someone to reassure you. But it can also be a mental ritual if you are repeatedly reviewing something in your head to get self-reassurance. We tend to look at hand washing as a common physical compulsion, and yet there are lots of mental review and other rituals happening in the mind before you decide to go to the sink. Although a compulsion can literally take any form, the following are some common compulsive responses seen in OCD that we will attempt to demystify.

Avoidance

In a way, all compulsions are a form of avoidance, an attempt to distance yourself from uncomfortable thoughts and feelings. Here let's discuss avoidance in a more specific context, and take a look at the literal act of trying not to be around something that triggers your OCD.

When we avoid something, we believe that we are sending a message from the mind to the brain that we are safe. But the brain uses an opposite language. It bases its calculations on its assessment of what you've chosen to do with your mind and body in response to the thoughts and feelings it presented. So when you avoid something, you aren't returning a message of safety; you are returning a message of narrowly escaped danger. If you avoid your coffee cup, you aren't learning that you are safe from coffee; you are learning that coffee cups are dangerous.

In the case of physical avoidance, you may be avoiding a perceived contaminant by not using household cleaning products, public restrooms, and so on. Or you may be avoiding shaking hands or touching doorknobs. None of this is necessarily making you safe. It's just making the avoided thing appear to be dangerous.

While avoidance of things in the physical world can occur on a range from avoiding eye contact to avoiding going outside at all, it's our avoidance of thoughts and feelings that really keeps the OCD machine revving. By trying to avoid having certain thoughts and feelings, you are blocking yourself from using mindfulness as a tool against OCD. You may avoid items, people, or places that you perceive to be contaminated or triggering because of your OCD. You may avoid activities that could bring on feared thoughts, such as driving, cooking, exercising, or socializing.

Take a moment to write down any avoidance you engage in as a result of your OCD. You may want to cross-reference this list with the notes you wrote in the previous chapter while constructing your hierarchy:

_____

_____

_____

Washing Compulsions

At some time in relatively recent human history, we began rubbing soap on our skin and rinsing it off with water. This probably solved a few problems, but in the case of OCD, it's the source of a lot of suffering for the compulsive washer. The idea behind a washing ritual is that you are somehow going from *dirty* (which you may find unacceptable) to *clean* (which you may find essential).

Washing compulsions often correlate to contamination obsessions: fears of getting or spreading germs or diseases. But they can also be a response to a fear of just feeling *off* or emotionally *unclean*, independently of whether you are thinking about specific contaminants. Washing can also be a completely indirect ritual, such as washing in response to an intrusive sexual or violent thought in an attempt to feel that you have somehow neutralized its presence in your mind with a cleansing act. It can also be about symmetry and numbers, rewashing so as to ensure that a washing ritual ended on the "right" note.

Hand Washing

Compulsive hand washing can be an issue of frequency, duration, or both. You may be doing very quick, very simple washes but feel that you must do them several times throughout the day for a variety of reasons. Or you may have a series of steps that you must follow precisely to achieve the "right" feeling. This can go on for hours, often resulting in severe skin damage and infections, not to mention interpersonal conflicts, brutal self-esteem hits, and practical loss of time.

Practice: As a mindfulness practice, pay particular attention to the individual steps of your next hand washing, and then write them down here or on a separate sheet of paper. Even if you don't struggle with compulsive hand washing, this can be an eye-opening exercise in everyday ritualistic behavior.

_____

_____

_____

If you have been a compulsive hand washer for some time, you may feel that you cannot trust yourself to wash noncompulsively because you have difficulty remembering what that looks like. Don't be ashamed if this is the case, because it's quite common. You may be afraid that in your attempt to wash "normally," you will somehow do less than you *should*. Note how the OCD mind uses cognitive distortions here to keep you doing your compulsions.

In our experience with treating OCD sufferers, typical *noncompulsive* hand washing generally falls within these parameters:

- Hands are typically washed only at the following times:
  - when there are *visible* substances (such as dirt, paint, or blood)
  - after you use the restroom
  - before you eat

- Hand washing starts with soap, not a prerinse or prewash ritual.

- Hands are washed with water at a comfortable temperature that does not scald or irritate the skin.

- A moderate amount of soap is used, such as one to two pumps of liquid.

- Washing is not repeated after the initial rinse.

- Rinsing ends after soap is no longer readily visible.

- There's no counting involved.

- No scratching of the skin is involved.

- Washing doesn't extend beyond the wrists.

- Washing doesn't involve attention to individual fingers or nails, unless there's a specific thing being washed on a particular finger or nail (for example, you got ink from your pen on your thumb).

- Washing involves touching the faucet handle with your hands before *and* after the wash.

- Total washing lasts an amount of time that doesn't impair functioning or reduce quality of life

You may be thinking that the previous guidelines are difficult to follow. Don't expect that you will have to go from wherever your OCD has you now to these guidelines overnight. You can work on this process gradually, and you will find some more strategies in part 2 of this book. For now, write down the reasons you feel that you have to wash in your specific way:

_____

_____

_____

The Shower

The shower can be a tremendous source of stress for someone doing compulsions. Many people with OCD spend a significant portion of the shower experience washing their hands to try to keep the hands from cross-contaminating parts of the body that the OCD says are clean with parts of the body that the OCD says are dirty. You may even wash your loofah, the shampoo bottle, or the bar of soap itself. Counting and symmetry rituals are also very common in the shower. This may include washing quadrants of your body until they feel right and then repeating this behavior a certain number of times. Showering rituals may become so daunting that showering is avoided altogether.

Practice: As a mindfulness exercise, the next time you shower, pay close attention to each step and then write all of the steps down here, or on a separate sheet of paper. You will want to use this list to break down your showering compulsions when we approach the issue in part 2 of this workbook.

_____

_____

_____

Cleaning Your Environment

A common misconception about OCD sufferers is that they are neat and tidy. Although some people find their OCD pushing them to keep everything spotless, it's quite common for OCD to keep you *from* cleaning, because it's too burdensome to meet your own compulsive standards. You may have garbage in your home that can't be removed because it seems too contaminated to touch (or it may seem too burdensome to wash yourself after you touch it). Or there may be a variety of items that have been labeled *untouchable* for emotional reasons. It's hard to clean when you can't touch the things that need to be cleaned—even harder when you can't touch cleaning products!

But for those who have compulsive tendencies toward keeping everything ordered and tidy, this can be a very painful process of constantly checking to see what's "off" and what needs to be fixed. It may have little to do with cleanliness and might mostly serve to get the "feeling right." So cleaning becomes another form of avoiding unwanted thoughts and feelings.

Cleaning can also be used as a form of avoiding some other unwanted thought or feeling. For example, an OCD sufferer may have an intrusive thought about her religion or a violent or sexual thought, and might start engaging in very methodical cleaning rituals as a way of distracting herself from the thoughts. This may also be a form of self-punishment for having the thoughts.

You don't have to *be* a messy or dirty person overall to overcome OCD. But you do have to be *willing* to do some of the things that may make you feel messy or dirty, and to sit with the experience this elicits. If cleaning is a compulsion for you, describe what you clean and what your motivations are when they go beyond making something look nice:

_____

_____

_____

_____

Checking

Checking is a compulsion designed to force a sense of safety when safety is mostly an illusion anyway. When a person locks a door or shuts off a stove, he typically walks away from the experience feeling as if he has accomplished some minor task. The door *feels* locked, and the stove *feels* shut off. This person doesn't have OCD. So his brain presents his mind with whatever sensation equated to "Got it done; on to the next thing." Someone with OCD who engages in checking rituals isn't getting that message. She is waiting for it and scanning the mind for it, but finding nothing, she determines that the task might not have been completed. So she goes back and checks. And she does it over and over and over again until she forces her brain to produce the sensation of completion—at least long enough to get out of the house and far enough away not to turn back.

It has been suggested that OCD sufferers who engage in this type of checking compulsion have a deficit in the nonverbal memory center of the brain that leads them to feel unclear when something has been completed, unless it has been spoken (Cha et al. 2008). But other researchers suspect that the problem is more likely a result of checking compulsions being used in response to a mistrust of one's memory, not a deficit in the memory itself (Moritz et al. 2006).

The brain is a learning machine, so it's watching this checking behavior and learning that, in the absence of the sense of completion, you are willing to engage in a repeated behavior that will force that sensation to occur. Therefore, the brain stops putting any effort into providing that at which it was already doing an inefficient job. That part of the brain that tells the mind, *Okay, we're done here; move on*, sort of goes into atrophy. This means you have to do more and more checking rituals to get the same effect.

Checkers typically check things that they associate with catastrophes, even when those catastrophes are no more likely to occur than getting struck by lightning—checking to ensure that coffee machines are off, for example, because of the fear that the building will catch fire from a coffee machine that was left on. The fact that the hot plate on a coffee machine doesn't just burst into flames seems blocked from the OCD mind. So what the checker is left with is a never-ending state of slavery to the checking compulsion. The more you check, the less confident you feel in your ability to accomplish tasks, so the more you have to check.

Checking may involve physically touching an item, visually observing the item, or mentally reviewing whether the item has been checked. Mindfulness for checking means acknowledging that you had an urge to check, a thought about an item going unchecked, and a feeling that something isn't the way it's supposed to be. Acknowledging these things, accepting them, and choosing to move forward anyway, *away* from checking, is essential for overcoming OCD.

What are some things that you feel compelled to check?

_____

_____

_____

How do you feel before you decide to check?

\

Mental Checking

It's not just about going back to make sure the stove is off. The physical act of returning to check is often a last-ditch effort to neutralize the discomfort that comes with unwanted thoughts about unchecked things bursting into flames (literally or figuratively). This means that a mountain of mental checking must be happening first. Whenever you try to answer the question in your head, *Is it done?* you are engaging in a mental ritual. Checking your mind doesn't help you know whether it's done. The mind has no new information.

Mental checking is also very common with feelings and physical sensations. If you struggle with contamination OCD, you may check mentally to see if you *feel* clean enough. If you struggle with obsessions about violence, sexual thoughts, or morality, you might repeatedly check to see if the emotions you are having in response to an event are appropriate. Like physical checking, it's typically a brief, but repeated, act of returning to a scene. Just as you might check your watch noncompulsively to see if you are on time, you might, from compulsion, *mentally* check an idea to make sure it's where it belongs in your mind.

Here are some common things that someone with OCD might mentally check:

- Whether emotions are appropriate to an event

- A mental image of a locked door or a shut light switch, and so on

- A sensation in the groin in the presence of a sexual obsession

- Whether a belief still seems valid

What types of things do you mentally check?

\

Mental Review

What did I say? What did they mean? Where was I when that happened? How did I feel? These questions come up a lot in OCD, and you have to drop mindfulness to answer them because they require delving into an imaginary past. Whereas mental checking is looking to see whether something is the way the OCD says it should be, *mental review* is studying and analyzing it.

This compulsion is also called *ruminating*, and for good reason. When an animal, such as a cow, digests food, it chews it, swallows it, digests it a bit, vomits it back up, chews it again, and completes digesting it. This vomiting is called "ruminating." It's appropriate, if not somewhat disgusting, as a way of describing the OCD mental process of regurgitating a thought or feeling in an attempt to further digest it.

Mental review is an attempt to examine the past with the objective of letting it go. This is sometimes referred to as "rewinding the tape," because it's the mental equivalent of studying a scene over and over. Since the sufferer believes that reviewing the event (interaction, conversation, statement, and so on) will resolve it and subsequently reduce uncomfortable thoughts and feelings, it's a compulsion. Unfortunately, mental review, like other compulsions, doesn't really work. There's no "aha!" moment that let's you off the hook. The closer you get to thinking you've resolved the obsession, the higher OCD simply raises the standard by which you define "resolution."

The complicating factor of this compulsion is that the act of recalling a memory fundamentally distorts that memory. When you have an experience, you are having it in the present moment, along with all of the thoughts and feelings and physical sensations that are co-occurring. When you review an experience, you are reviewing it from *this* present moment. That means it's a version of the past, not the actual past experience. OCD takes advantage of this by pushing you to review and review again, in hopeless attempts to get closer and closer to a mythical certainty about what happened. But it's impossible to attain this certainty. It simply doesn't exist. And the repeated digging in your head only makes you feel further and further from the truth of what happened. Here are some commonly reviewed experiences for people with OCD:

- Conversations

- Driving routes

- Trains of thought

- Reading material

- Specific events

What are some examples of times when you typically notice that you are mentally reviewing?

_____

_____

Scenario Bending

The mental ritual of *scenario bending* (also known as *theorizing* or *hypothesizing*) combines reviewing and checking by first replaying an event that *did* take place and then adding a hypothetical element of the event that *could have happened but did not* take place. Someone engaging in this compulsion would then proceed to analyze how he *would* have behaved if the feared scenario *had* taken place. The ritual is aimed at determining how appropriately you would respond in a feared hypothetical scenario, in the hopes that you will have certainty of your moral constitution.

Because the OCD knows that this is all theater but you may *feel* it's an honest attempt to work out a mental construct, the result is typically some sense of ambiguity about what you would or wouldn't do. Your OCD then uses this as evidence that you are morally defective, and that the obsessions are warnings that you must take very seriously.

Do you play out scenarios in your head and try to guess what you would do to feel more certain about something? Describe your process here:

_____

_____

_____

Mental Rehearsal

While mental review often involves replaying the past, *mental rehearsal*, or *reverse ruminating*, involves replaying invented visions of the future, in an attempt to check for the likelihood of catastrophe. Unlike scenario bending, which starts with the present moment and reviews what could have occurred, reverse ruminating takes place entirely in the future: at an upcoming performance, encounter, interview, or other event that could go terribly wrong.

This is often confused with simply *preparing*, but it's better described as compulsively going over and over something that has yet to happen, in an attempt to relieve discomfort about what *could* happen. This might come in the form of repeating potential conversations in your head before a date or a meeting with the boss. While a non-OCD sufferer could do this once or twice to help boost confidence, you may be looking for certainty that you will have a future experience precisely as you want it, rather than accepting that the future may bring any number of things to the present to be dealt with.

When do you notice that you are rehearsing feared future events?

_____

_____

_____

Reassurance Seeking

OCD sufferers often fail to identify reassurance seeking as a compulsion (Williams et al. 2011). After all, if you have doubts about something, particularly something that you view as extremely important, it seems reasonable to get a second opinion. But like checking, reassurance seeking doesn't stop the loop in your head for more than a moment. It just creates a new loop. You had an obsessive thought and found some way of feeling that it was addressed, and now every time you have that obsessive thought, you feel that it has to be addressed in that way! Many compulsions are varying forms of reassurance seeking. If you are washing, you are trying to reassure yourself that you are clean, as an alternative to accepting the uncertainty that you may be contaminated. If you are asking someone whether your thoughts are normal, you are trying to get reassurance that it's okay to have the thoughts you are having.

The most difficult challenge with reassurance seeking is the way in which it doubles up on itself. If someone assures you that the item you touched won't make you sick, you then want reassurance that that person knows what she's talking about. If you can get reassurance that she is an expert in what makes people sick, you want reassurance that she's telling you the truth and not just trying to appease you. Furthermore, either answer to your questions simply fuels more of the OCD behavior. If you get the feared answer, your anxiety goes up, and you want more reassurance that everything will be okay. If you get the answer that brings relief, you've only just validated the asking, ensuring that you will have to ask every time your obsessive thought returns.

Reassurance seeking may come in several different forms:

- Asking someone about your obsession

- Researching the obsession

- Confessing (letting someone know that you are having an obsessive thought in order to manipulate that person into telling you it's okay)

- Engaging in self-reassurance (using mental review or other rituals to reconfirm that your fears are unfounded)

One thing that seems to be very helpful with family members and partners is the formation of a reassurance contract. Simply put, the person with OCD gives permission for a loved one to refuse reassurance or to reduce it to a bare minimum. When the individual asks for reassurance, the family member participating in the contract can say something like, "Remember, you asked me to help you, and that means I can't answer this question. Now let's go do something else." This can literally be done by writing up an actual contract, sharing it with the reassurance giver, and having both of you sign it.

Another strategy that can be helpful is to start to reduce your seeking of vocal reassurance by agreeing to put all compulsive questions and confessions in a written format that your significant other or partner in treatment will review and respond to in a "reassurance book." You can then gradually reduce the entries over time. It may be important to include professional guidance with this technique, because it's essentially allowing a compulsion to take place as you gradually minimize it.

Use the following space to write down the different sources (people, websites, and so on) that you normally use for reassurance, and what strategies you employ to get it:

_____

_____

Thought Neutralization

This compulsion involves silently saying words or purposely attending to thoughts that are the opposite of the unwanted OCD thoughts. The belief is that a "good" thought will neutralize a "bad" one, and preempt unwanted consequences. For example, you might respond to the thought *I might hurt that person* with *I love that person.*

This can come up in any form of OCD and is an act of nonmindfulness in the extreme. It's an attempt not only to deny the presence of an unwanted thought and block the mind from accepting what it's receiving, but also to manipulate the mind into believing it's actually receiving something else! It's not a guide to rational, objective thinking, as in cognitive therapy, but a ruse to the mind. Mindfulness approaches to OCD need to involve rejection of the thought neutralization concept. It's inherently nonacceptant. How can a thought be neutralized if, by its very nature, it's a *thought,* and thus fundamentally neutral anyway until acted upon? If thought neutralizing is a strategy you've used to deal with unwanted thoughts, write down some examples here:

_____

_____

_____

_____

_____

In regard to thought neutralization, mindfulness specifically means acknowledging that your mind has received a thought and that because of the content of this thought, you are experiencing an urge to undo it or replace it with its opposite. So you will need to observe the initial triggering thought as well as the subsequent urge to neutralize. Watch these two events occur without engaging either of them, and you will see them both decrease over time.

Hoarding

With the publication of the *Diagnostic and Statistical Manual of Mental Disorders* (*DSM-5*) in 2013, the compulsion of hoarding is now classified as its own disorder; however, it's also commonly assessed as both an obsession and a compulsion in OCD (Frost and Hristova 2011). Hoarding means that you are keeping or taking in significantly more than you are physically removing from your life, and in extreme cases this can lead to major health risks, financial problems, or other risks (such as fire hazards).

You may find that you have difficulty letting go of things, and they may range from the sentimental (such as an old toy) to the somewhat nonsensical (like a gum wrapper). The OCD mind receives a thought about the value of the item or the consequence of removing it, and you simply cling to that item. You may be thinking it's something that you will reference one day and be glad you kept it, or you may be thinking that the emotional discomfort of parting with it is more than you can tolerate.

Hoarding is not collecting. For it to be considered hoarding, it must be problematic, adding chaos and stress to your life. If you engage in hoarding, what types of things do you have difficulty letting go of?

_____

_____

Memory Hoarding

Memory hoarding is a mental compulsion to overattend to the details of an event, person, or object in an attempt to mentally store it for safekeeping. This is generally done under the belief that the event, person, or object carries a special significance and will be important to recall exactly "as is" at a later date. The memory serves the same function for the mental hoarder that the old newspaper serves for the physical hoarder. An OCD sufferer doing memory hoarding may be concerned that moments in time will pass without his fully understanding, remembering, and appreciating them. The uncertainty surrounding whether or not he will be able to adequately reflect upon and evaluate the significance of specific events, people, or objects causes discomfort, which he hopes to avoid.

Mindfulness and Compulsions

It's somewhat like that "last look" you take the moment you leave an apartment from which you have just finished moving all the boxes. You stop, you consider that this is the last time you will be this person in this place, and then you move on to the next chapter in life.

If you are engaging in memory hoarding, it's likely that you feel trapped in a state of never fully being able to take in the true value of this moment. The twisted irony of memory hoarding is that by trying to perfectly remember things, you frequently miss out on really experiencing those very things! When we don't allow ourselves to be present in the moment, we are losing a great deal of the value of life in the process.

If you engage in memory hoarding, what's the process like for you?

_____

_____

_____

_____

_____

Symmetry Compulsions

For some people with OCD, there's a very strong pull toward repeating behaviors in an attempt to make things feel equal. If one shoelace is hanging longer than another, it can be difficult to just leave it that way. If one sideburn is shorter than another, it can take hours to get them exactly right.

A common compulsion might be to touch something or tap something solely because something else was touched or tapped and you were left with a feeling that something was off. Mindfulness asks that we tolerate this off feeling and stay present with it until it inevitably goes away. OCD says, *No, fix it. Fix it now, or you'll suffer forever.* So you end up touching your right knee because you accidentally touched your left knee, tapping a floor tile because your foot accidentally tapped one just to the right of it, turning to look at one wall because you happened to become aware that you had turned to look at the other one, and so on.

73

If symmetry or exactness compulsions play a role in your OCD, use the following space to write down how you fix things to make them feel complete:

_____

_____

Compulsive Flooding

As a behavioral technique, flooding can be an effective form of short-term exposure with response prevention for an unwanted thought (see the discussion in the previous chapter). It would typically take the shape of agreeing with and exaggerating the thought until habituation sets in and mindfulness can return. Sometimes sufferers who engage in a lot of obsessional thinking will use this technique as a form of *testing* their reactions to situations, and force themselves to flood unwanted thoughts in specific circumstances. Because it's painful, it demonstrates to you that the thoughts are somehow not really yours. For example, if you fear harming someone, you may force yourself to imagine committing an act of violence. The thought disgusts and horrifies you, so then you review *how* horrified you are and use this as a strategy for feeling more assured that you wouldn't commit such an act.

If something triggers you, the mindful approach would be to observe the thoughts, feelings, and urges that come up in response to the trigger. One of these urges may be to make it worse, not in an attempt to do exposure but for the purpose of checking and self-reassuring.

What are situations where you compulsively force yourself to think the worst?

_____

_____

Self-Punishment

Both OCD sufferers and treatment providers often overlook the compulsion to exact mental abuse against oneself. You may believe that you have done something wrong or committed some sort of unforgivable error. Or in OCD terms, you may struggle with uncertainty about potential past transgressions. To accept that you *might* have done the wrong thing and move on would mean tolerating the discomfort of feeling as if you were getting away with a crime (whether the crime actually happened or not). To account for this, you may intentionally force feelings of guilt and negative self-thoughts as a form of sentencing for the crime, just in case. Once you feel adequately punished, you believe that you are more likely to move on.

While beating yourself up is obviously painful, it's a relief strategy from the greatest pain you can imagine: escaping justice. Self-punishment may seem like the responsible thing to do, but it's ultimately still a way of avoiding the acceptance of uncertainty. It may take many forms, from engaging in negative self-talk to forcing yourself to endure more compulsions. What forms of self-punishment do you engage in because of your OCD?

_____

_____

Compulsive Prayer

If you have obsessive thoughts about your religious faith (see chapter 13, on scrupulosity OCD), prayer is often used to counteract the intrusion of antireligious or otherwise unacceptable thoughts. Prayer becomes unhealthy ritual when it's used repeatedly to neutralize thoughts or evade them, rather than as an attempt to more genuinely connect with one's religious faith.

When you engage in compulsive prayer, you are concurrently checking the validity of your prayers so that you are never really present with the prayer. The prayer never feels quite complete, so repetition and other rituals set in. This makes you feel further from your faith, not closer, and it doubles back on itself. The more compulsive prayer you engage in, the more blasphemous you feel, so the more you pray. Prayer may also be used compulsively in an attempt to neutralize uncomfortable thoughts and feelings related to other obsessions. If you pray, are there ways in which you do so compulsively?

_____

_____

Counting

Counting can be its own compulsion, in which you feel the need to count to keep something bad from happening, or it can be used as a form of compulsive avoidance, such as when you count to distract yourself from the presence of other unwanted thoughts.

Many people experience counting not as a compulsion, but as a benign obsession. In other words, the counting of steps, tiles, or anything else is just *happening*. These people aren't doing it with any goal in mind. The problem is that they are aware that they are counting, and they feel annoyed by it. This has obvious parallels to other benign obsessions, like breathing and blinking. (See chapter 14 for further discussion.) But in the case of counting, it can sometimes present like something that's just going on. The compulsion then is to wish that it were *not* going on and to dwell on the annoyance, rather than accept that counting is occurring. The same approach would be necessary for the awareness of any repeated thought whose content is not the issue so much as its mere presence (for example, getting songs stuck in your head). Does counting play a role in your OCD? How?

_____

_____

Mindfulness for Compulsions

Mindfulness helps us to resist compulsions, because it allows us to see where the seed of the compulsion is planted. It starts with the presence of the uncomfortable thought, feeling, or physical sensation. And somewhere in that space between our awareness of the obsession and our decision to compulsively respond lies mindfulness. Mindfulness for compulsions is the art of waiting. Just as you sit in the lobby of your therapist's office and wait for her to call you in, you sit and wait in your mind. When the OCD calls you in, you say, *Oh, I'm here for something else*. When the *present* calls you in, you go willingly toward it.

When we resist compulsions, whether it's resisting mental review, washing, avoiding, or reassurance seeking, we are accepting uncertainty. Maybe you should have done that compulsion. Maybe as a result of your failure to do the compulsion, the sky *will* fall. Maybe the sky falling is what you need to get your freedom back.

For every compulsion you resist, there's OCD payback. This payback usually comes in the form of extreme emotional pain. It doesn't matter if you resisted the compulsive response to a disgusting harm thought, or resisted touching the faucet one more time to get the number right. The pain is the same. Mindfulness is about seeing that pain land on your satellite and accepting it with open arms. Let it wash over you. Let it be rain that slips across you and down a gutter, instead of snow that builds and builds until you are crushed and buried.

Let your fear of resisting compulsions be replaced by a curiosity with what's on the other side.

Take a Breather

You may feel somewhat overwhelmed right now. Preparing to treat your OCD typically starts with a massive injection of information and a lot of talk about what you will be expected to do—all stuff that probably terrifies you! Take a moment to check in with yourself and notice what you are feeling. Don't try to convince yourself that everything will be all right. You don't know that. It may be all right. We know what the status quo has to offer. Don't leave the *now* for the purpose of assessing how mindfulness and CBT will help you *later*. Stay with whatever feelings you are having and offer yourself the willingness to turn the page into part 2. But don't frame it as, *Okay, now I have to do part 2*. Let yourself stay with the next page and see it for what it is—just the next page.

PART 2

Mindfulness and CBT for Specific Obsessions

I n this part, we will look at mindfulness, cognitive, and behavioral strategies for addressing different manifestations of OCD.

CHAPTER 5

Acceptance, Assessment, Action

I n the first part of this book, we looked at three main areas of interest in the treatment of OCD. First, we examined mindfulness, and how acceptance of thoughts, feelings, and sensations can bring about a greater capacity to resist compulsive urges. Then we looked at cognitive therapy and how your assessing the argument from your OCD that so often leads to compulsions can help you identify distorted thinking. Then we looked at behavioral therapy tools and how you can use them to take action, facing your fears head-on and overcoming them through a technique called "exposure with response prevention." In the pages ahead, we hope to simplify and illuminate these three strategies of accepting, assessing, and taking action to overcome your OCD.

Acceptance

Acceptance means using mindful awareness to shift your perspective and accept the presence of OCD thoughts and feelings.

The mindfulness approach comes down to one global rule: to fully accept that the thoughts that are going through your head are indeed the thoughts that are going through your head. It means dropping any denial that what you are thinking is anything other than what you are thinking. Compulsions are strategies for resisting the experience you are having, whether it be an experience of thought, emotion, or anything else. So mindfulness is the anticompulsion, the antiresistance.

You may find that you struggle with the word "accept" when you are applying it to your OCD. Although the thoughts cause you great pain, accepting them means accepting that they are a part of you, that it *could* mean something. We don't want to accept them. We want them to go away! But the great con we play against OCD is that by accepting our thoughts as thoughts, feelings as feelings, and so on, we are actually allowing them to go *through* us rather than get stuck inside us.

When you use compulsions to resist a feeling, like anxiety or fear, you aren't destroying that feeling. You are simply pushing it aside. Every time you experience OCD discomfort and push that experience aside, you are stacking it on top of the last one. So every time you are triggered, you deal with not only the experience you are having, but also the large stack of pain you've been building up. Practicing mindfulness by choosing acceptance as the first response is how you can take some of that pain off the stack and start dealing with problems as they are in the moment.

Acceptance doesn't mean defeat, and it doesn't mean that what you are accepting is the *meaning* behind the content of your thoughts. What you are accepting is merely that those are the thoughts that your mind is receiving from your brain. So to effectively use mindfulness for OCD, always start with acceptance, and whatever other techniques you use to address the OCD, return to acceptance immediately thereafter.

To fully accept a thought, you have to be willing to accept that the thought *may* have meaning. This doesn't *give* the thought meaning. To the contrary, this liberates you from having to be certain. So when presented with an intrusive thought, start by using mindfulness to take an observational, nonjudgmental stance toward what's happening. *I'm having a thought about being contaminated* is a much different experience from *I'm contaminated, and I'll die if I don't wash right away!*

From the nonjudgmental stance, you can maintain clarity, and from clarity you can determine whether or not the compulsions you would normally choose are ultimately in your best interest. You can see the discomfort that comes from not doing the compulsion, but you can also see that discomfort fade away. Then you can see the sense of victory that comes from knowing that you were able to override the demands of your OCD.

Assessment

Assessment means using cognitive therapy skills to assess the value of an intrusive OCD thought or feeling for the purpose of returning to the present.

Acceptance is hard. It's not as simple as stretching out your arms and welcoming your thoughts. It's the work of breaking down resistance to thoughts, and sometimes the effort that takes can be overwhelming. It can reduce you to tears, to depression, to not wanting to try to fight. So sometimes it's necessary to step back and assess the situation to better determine how important it really is for you to do your compulsions. It's as if your mind is stuck with the opinion that you cannot tolerate the discomfort and must do a compulsion, so you are getting a second opinion from *yourself*. This is where cognitive therapy tools come in.

Remember that assessment of the obsession is *not* designed to prove the thoughts or feelings untrue or safe. The point here is simply to help you guide yourself away from the compulsive response. If the thought is *I'll get a disease from touching that public pay phone* and you are able to restructure that to *Public pay phones make me uncomfortable, but in my experience, I've never gotten sick as a result of touching one*, then you are less likely to engage in compulsive behavior.

You can practice your assessment tools with thought records, or just by observing the types of cognitive distortions your mind tends to engage in with each OCD moment. Thoughts and feelings are not evidence. Evidence is evidence, and if you don't have it, observe how you are responding without it. You still have to accept that you may be wrong, but at least you can point yourself away from OCD-fueling compulsions. Then, with the thoughts assessed for distortions, you can go back to acceptance. You *had* that thought. Now back to the present.

Action

Action means using behavioral therapy skills to actively confront and expose yourself to OCD thoughts and feelings for the purpose of habituating to and overcoming your fears.

As you probably well know, assessing for the rationale in your OCD experience doesn't always produce results. Powerful discomfort may persist, and the urge to act on compulsions may continue to rain down hard. So if you have tried to accept the obsessive thought and let it go through you, and you have tried to assess the obsessive thought to guide it along, the next step is to take action toward freeing yourself from fear. This is where you use your behavioral therapy tools. Through the various forms of exposure with response prevention, you are taking action toward better mental health.

Categorizing Obsessions

Anyone has the capacity to think of anything, which means that anyone has the capacity to develop obsessions about anything. The categorizing of specific obsessions may at times seem dehumanizing. We are all just struggling with uncertainty about this or that and doing compulsions to make us feel safe. You may not want to identify yourself as a "washer" or someone with harm OCD and so on. In fact, labeling your OCD as being a special *kind* of OCD can make mindfulness more challenging, because it implies that thoughts have different qualities from one another, rather than that they are just thoughts.

The reason we separate obsessions into categories is that for every obsessive-compulsive cycle, there's a way to break it. There's a way *in*, and knowing the way in is important. When you understand the mechanics of an obsession and can identify the compulsions that hold it in place, you can begin the process of letting both of them go.

CHAPTER 6

Contamination OCD

If you are suffering from a fear of contamination, then you are most certainly tired of being told that you wash your hands too much or that your showers are too long. People are quick to criticize you for all the wasted soap and water, and that there are people without enough to eat who have "real" things to worry about. What they don't understand, unless they also have OCD, is that you are simply doing what you feel you have to do to survive. Letting yourself be contaminated seems like no more of an option than letting yourself be strangled or drowned. And yet, part of you knows that you are asking more of yourself than others are, that everything is already contaminated anyway somehow, and that your attempts to avoid being a part of that are hardly making the mere *feeling* of safety worth it.

When we use the term *contamination OCD*, we are typically referring to sufferers who are concerned that one item that they see as unacceptably *unclean* will cause other things to become unclean (including themselves) and that they are responsible for making sure this does not occur.

Additionally, some clients have a variation of contamination OCD that could be called *disgust OCD*, in which the primary focus isn't on germs or dirt or cleanliness, but on the feeling of disgust they experience when exposed to certain stimuli. In fact, research has suggested that an elevated disgust response is associated with OCD (Brady, Adams, and Lohr 2010) and that for some sufferers, an impaired disgust response can improve with CBT (Rector et al. 2012).

Typical triggers for contamination OCD sufferers include:

- Items used by the public (doorknobs, light switches, buses)

- Fecal matter (including things that are near fecal matter, such as toilets or parts of the body)

- Blood (or anything that could be near blood or cause blood to appear, including needles, bandages, doctor's offices)

- Other bodily fluids (urine, sweat, saliva, semen, vaginal secretions)

- Poison (or anything perceived as poisonous, including household cleaning agents; medicine; expired food; and environmental contaminants, such as asbestos, X-rays, pesticides, and chemicals)

- Alcohol or other drugs (especially for anyone recovering from addiction)

- Anything associated with illness (sick people, the homeless, hospitals)

- Anything to which you have a strong disgust response, without any specific concerns about illness, germs, and so forth (for example, substances that are sticky, wet, or just "unknown")

Use the following space to write down any specific things that prompt you to feel the need to avoid them, or wash your hands after you come in contact with them. (You may want to review the items you wrote down in the "Avoidance" section of chapter 4.)

_____

_____

_____

_____

_____

It's often presumed that the contamination OCD sufferer is highly concerned with germs and getting sick, and is attempting to obtain certainty that she won't get sick. Although this is a common experience for many OCD sufferers, there are actually several reasons someone with contamination OCD might avoid being triggered, including:

☐ Fear of getting sick or diseased from germs or viruses

☐ Fear of having to do extensive washing rituals

☐ Fear of spreading germs to others

☐ Fear of the feeling of disgust

☐ Fear of later feeling avoidant of valued items that you have touched

☐ Fear of being viewed as irresponsible or "dirty" by others

☐ Fear of becoming an irresponsible or "dirty" person

Check off any of the previous fears you relate to and write down in the following space any other reasons you may feel the urge to avoid or wash. If you are unclear about what triggers you or don't know exactly how to articulate it, then use the following space to write some of the themes that lead you to compulsive washing:

_____

_____

_____

_____

_____

Common compulsions found in contamination OCD include:

• Specific washing and cleaning rituals

• Avoidance of things viewed as contaminated, or avoidance of clean things when you feel contaminated

• Mental review of whether contact has been made with contaminants and whether washing rituals were properly executed.

- Asking others for reassurance that they have not been exposed to a contaminant or have not exposed others to contaminants

- Memory hoarding of contact with contaminants

What are some of the compulsions you act on because of your contamination fears?

_____

_____

_____

Acceptance Tools in Contamination OCD

To begin constructing your mindfulness-based approach to treating your contamination obsessions, you will need to start by being a student of your present experience with contaminants. Imagine that you have come in contact with something that you believe is contaminated. It happens in an instant. You touched something, maybe you were just near it, or maybe you aren't certain what was touched. Immediately your thoughts, feelings, and physical sensations start presenting you with information. Your mind is receiving a lot of signals at once, all of them with the potential to be very upsetting if you take them seriously. First, you become very aware of the part of your body that you think is contaminated. If you focus your attention on that part of the body, you will certainly notice that, as a function of overattention, you begin to get some sort of physical response. Your hands *feel* dirty to you.

Mindfulness suggests that you sit with that feeling, rather than attempt to destroy it. *Destroying* the feeling with compulsions sends the message to the brain that the feeling is your enemy. *Owning* the feeling sends the message that it's simply an experience, like many others, and that it doesn't warrant a massive amount of attention. Consider which message will result in less perpetuation of your obsessive-compulsive cycle.

So the first challenge has to do with how much attention you will give to the thoughts, feelings, and physical sensations you associate with being contaminated in this present moment. If you give them *all* of your attention, they will create a feedback loop of overvaluing and overresponding that's sure to drive you back to the sink or shower. If you give them *less* attention, this will bring about other thoughts and feelings, particularly ones related to irresponsibility and self-judgment. But what if you knew that these feelings were on their way and that they were exactly that, just *feelings*?

What if you were able to exist *with* the feeling of irresponsibility and allow yourself to see the bigger picture? The bigger picture is that no amount of washing ever gets you "clean," because your definition of the word "clean" necessarily involves experiencing a specific *feeling* that you call "clean." A computerized device that could measure germs wouldn't be enough. You would have to feel clean to be clean. But if you abandon that *clean* feeling and are being mindful of, and ultimately doing exposure with, the *feeling* of irresponsibility (or disgust, risk, and so on), you get the upper hand on the OCD.

Staying Present with Contamination Fears

When you feel contaminated or when you become focused on the idea that you or something or someone you care about is contaminated, you experience an urge to leave the present. The problem is, the more you flee the present feeling, the more space you give for the OCD to overpower you. If you flee to the past, you review what you think you might have touched, you fail to obtain the certainty you seek, and you feel more contaminated. If you flee to the future, you create imaginary negative fantasies of the contaminant spreading from one thing you care about to the next, and then you feel more responsible to prevent that and, thus, more contaminated! So leaving the present state of contamination always results in your feeling more contaminated.

Be Mindful of What You Are Mindful of When Washing

Practicing mindfulness in the moment is generally considered a good thing. In many books on mindfulness, you might find that the shower or the sink can be an excellent place to practice mindfulness. You are encouraged to pay attention to the way the soap feels against your skin, the sound of the water as it descends upon you, the warmth of the steam in the air, and so on. This is a great idea when no rituals are involved and the mindful attention is genuine. However, if you have contamination OCD with shower or hand-washing rituals, you might be paying attention to the present moment only for the purpose of making sure you don't miss anything. Paying too much attention to what's going on in this type of situation is half the problem!

A good, noncompulsive shower is chaos. It's throwing soap on your body and letting soap fall from your body. In this case, to get the upper hand on the OCD, you need to shower mindlessly, with less attention to detail, less order, less sense of ritual, and less awareness of what touched what and when. Instead, direct your mindfulness skills intentionally *away* from the physical body and toward the experience of uncertainty that comes from not paying attention to the shower. Focus your attention on the discomfort that comes from *not* ritualizing, from letting your mind wander instead of being consumed by details of which body part to wash and when.

Let these same rules apply to hand washing. Actually let yourself *do* some mental review or mental rehearsal of whatever could exist outside of the washing. Just don't let the mental review or rehearsal focus on the issue of contamination. What new song do you want to buy for your workout later? What was the best scene in the show you watched last night? Let the washing happen without the ritualizing. Then, after you have dried and are ready to move on, bring yourself back to the present and sit with the feeling of incompleteness. Notice the urge to review the wash for compulsive completeness. Turn the mindfulness back on. Come back to your body as it is.

> **Practice**: What thoughts, feelings, physical sensations, or other internal data do you believe you will need to mindfully accept while you relieve your contamination OCD?

Meditation Tips for Contamination OCD

If you choose to use daily meditation as part of your mindfulness training for OCD, consider what types of thoughts, feelings, and physical sensations you may find pulling you away from the present. As you breathe and attend to that breath, you may notice the OCD sending you signals to attend to something that you may believe you have touched earlier. Nod to that thought; tell yourself, *Hey, look at that thought about having touched something. Okay, I can have that thought with me as I focus on my breath.* Maybe you begin to lose focus in your meditation and feel an urge to analyze or otherwise address some feeling of being contaminated. Try to observe the feeling as simply something else that's present in that moment. Don't go into problem-solving mode. The ground beneath you, the air temperature, the sounds outside your window—these things are all present with you as you attend to your breathing. You don't mind them. Let the feeling of being contaminated be just another thing that's present as you attend to your breath. Remember, you are exercising the muscle of not minding.

Assessment Tools for Contamination OCD

Cognitive restructuring, enhanced by mindfulness, can be very effective for contamination OCD. The important element is maintaining a stance that your thoughts about contamination may still be true. However—and it's a *big* "however"—your reasoning and your evidence supporting the urge to wash or avoid is insufficient. It may not be enough for you to simply say, *Well, I feel a bit contaminated, but I'll just sit with it and not wash for now.* You might need the extra push of an objective assessment of the washing urge. This is where identifying distorted thinking and breaking it apart come in.

First and foremost, all-or-nothing thinking drives the very idea of contamination and decontamination: *I'm either clean or dirty. If I have washed correctly, I'm clean. If I haven't washed, I'm dirty until I wash.* This way of thinking hands over all the power to the OCD. OCD defines what's contaminated, and arbitrarily changes its definition to whatever will make you do compulsions, so that life becomes mostly about waiting for the next contaminant. Challenging this distortion necessitates acknowledging that you never know how dirty (or clean) something is, but it can never be 100 percent dirty (or clean).

Contamination OCD also combines emotional reasoning with catastrophizing to promote the idea that feeling contaminated means you *are* contaminated and that staying contaminated means you will spread it: *I know I'm dirty, because I feel as if I came in contact with something dirty that must have gotten on me. I'm going to spread this contaminant everywhere if I don't wash now.* This is another example of how the OCD subverts mindfulness by making predictions and assumptions about the future. It's not only uncertain whether you are presently contaminated, but also impossible to know how being contaminated will affect you or the outside world at any point in the future. Again, the challenge is in identifying that a feeling of contamination is not a *fact* of contamination, and that a thought about spreading that contaminant is not a threat of spreading it.

Emotional reasoning can also make washing rituals especially challenging, because a large driver for continuing the ritual is waiting to *feel clean* or *right.* This is why washing rituals can be so time consuming. You might look down and see that you've washed your hands and even completed whatever other related ritual seemed necessary, but the *feeling* isn't there, so you keep going. Breaking the obsessive-compulsive cycle necessitates leaving the sink *without* the feeling you were shooting for, and accepting the discomfort that follows.

What cognitive distortions do you see as the most compelling for your contamination OCD? (You might want to review some of your notes from chapter 2.)

_____

_____

_____

_____

_____

Practice: Use an automatic thought record (see chapter 2) to challenge some of your distorted thoughts about contaminants. Remember that the goal is not to convince yourself that you are clean. It's to acknowledge and mindfully accept that you have very little to go on that justifies a compulsive decontamination ritual.

Sample Automatic Thought Record

Trigger What set you off?	Automatic Thought What is the OCD saying?	Challenge What is an alternative to the distorted thinking?
Saw red mark on wall.	There's blood on the wall, and if I don't avoid it by a great distance, it will get in me and I'll get HIV.	I don't know what the red mark is. I do know that this situation typically makes me very uncomfortable, but simply seeing it or being near it isn't the same thing as injecting it into my veins. In any case, I'm notorious for seeing red spots on things because of my HIV obsession, so this might just be one of those OCD challenges.

Action Tools for Contamination OCD

Exposure is a fundamental part of treating all forms of OCD, but nowhere is the in vivo, or direct contact, experience more important than in contamination OCD. This doesn't mean you have to (or should ever) force yourself to come in contact with anything actually dangerous. You must come in contact with your *fear*, and you can do this in a number of ways. You don't have to touch feces or blood or toxic chemicals to overcome a fear of being contaminated by these things. But you *do* need to be close enough to the thing you fear to *feel* contaminated. Without creating and habituating to the feeling of contamination, you remain a slave to your efforts to decontaminate.

Getting Close to Fear

Doing ERP for contamination-related fears involves a combination of increasing contact with, and decreasing *avoidance* of, things you perceive as contaminated. Consider that some contact with the world is necessary, and parts of the world are contaminated. So being alive means being in a place that may or may not be contaminated by what you fear. Your approach to *feeling* safe is to purposefully avoid touching things, and to carefully wash away whatever it is that you cannot be certain you avoided. So ERP essentially boils down to getting closer and closer to those things you fear, but it also involves breaking down your washing rituals into smaller, less compulsive parts.

In Vivo ERP for Contamination OCD

Start by making a list of all the things you fear being contaminated by. Note again that you should never put yourself in a situation where you are purposefully coming in contact with something dangerous. The goal is not to get pricked by a used hypodermic needle you found on the sidewalk! The goal is to be able to walk down the street where one may have been left behind and to keep enjoying the song you were listening to before you noticed it. So consider all of the items, people, and places you avoid, all of the things you check, and all of the things that trigger urges to wash. Here are a few examples for blood-related contamination compulsions:

- Avoiding rosebushes because thorns could cause cuts

- Checking skin for cuts or openings

- Avoiding the first-aid aisle of the grocery store (people with cuts buy bandages!)

- Avoiding all contact with shoes (they may have touched blood on the sidewalk somehow)

- Avoiding being near hospitals

- Looking carefully at items to ensure that they have no sharp edges

- Avoiding people you think are at higher risk of having HIV because of their ethnicity or sexual orientation

- Checking your car, clothes, or other items for evidence of blood

What are you avoiding because of your contamination OCD?

_____

_____

_____

_____

No matter how long your list may be, try to get all of your trigger items in one place and try to put them in order of least-to-most triggering. Then, starting with the most feasible item, start making contact with the things you avoid or start eliminating compulsive behaviors every day. Think about how it would make you feel to resist checking something before using it or to touch something like the floor and not wash until it was time to eat. Think about sitting with that feeling instead of eliminating it. You may wish to review "The Compulsive Hierarchy" section of chapter 3 for further guidance.

If you put your mindfulness skills to the test and choose to exist *with* that feeling, what are you ready for? Start there. It's fine if you're feeling afraid to make giant leaps into contamination exposures. Take tiny steps. Let yourself just start to gently push against the boundaries your OCD has laid out for you. Try one minor modification to your OCD routine, see how it feels, and see if you get a sense of mastery over it in time. If not, try something easier, and then go back to the more challenging exposures.

Walk Away Unclean

The most important thing to understand about ERP for contamination concerns is that if you are leaving the experience feeling clean, you are doing it wrong. You want to walk away from the shower, the sink, or wherever your decontamination rituals take place feeling imperfect, irresponsible, unclean, and *uncertain*. What is or isn't on your skin has nothing to do with what has taken over your life. The thing to master here is the entire experience of contamination, including thoughts about what's been touched and what it means, feelings of disgust and wretchedness, and even physical sensations of filthiness.

ERP is about creating that experience instead of fleeing from it, spending time with it instead of destroying it. Mindful awareness and acceptance of that experience will eventually turn it around and incorporate it into the larger picture of your life. This means that you will not only stop overattending, overvaluing, and overresponding to the notion of contamination, but also stop wondering when it will go away. Your life will be too interesting for you to be so easily distracted by something as transient as an idea of contamination.

Imaginal ERP for Contamination OCD

Imaginal exposure can be very helpful for confronting inaccessible or dangerous contaminants and for confronting fears related to morality and responsibility that might be pushing you to do contamination-related compulsions (review the section "Imaginal Exposure," in chapter 3, for the discussion on imaginal exposure tools). You can construct your own imaginal script for contamination concerns using the following activity. You might notice that this activity generates some amount of anxiety, and if it's too much for you to handle at this moment, again let yourself take a deep breath and just read the questions without answering them. Then, if you feel prepared to give it a shot, start filling in the answers at whatever level you believe you can tolerate.

What will you come in contact with?

_____

_____

What will happen if you fail to clean this item off of you completely?

_____

_____

How will this make you feel, and how will this feeling affect your behavior?

_____

_____

Who or what will become contaminated as a result of your inability to get clean?

_____

_____

How will other people be affected by becoming contaminated? What will they think of you for contaminating them? How will you feel about this?

_____

_____

What other efforts will you engage in to get clean, and what will happen when they fail?

_____

_____

What will the rest of your life look like if you remain contaminated?

_____

_____

_____

Remember, the goal of a script like this is to make enough contact with your discomfort to begin the process of accepting the discomfort. Once the feeling is no longer a threat to you, the urge to avoid your triggers will also decrease. This doesn't mean that you will suddenly become a person who doesn't care about your safety or the safety of others. What it means is that you will be able to make choices free of the influence of your OCD, and be able to see your thoughts and feelings for what they are rather than allowing them to bully you into a life of endless ritual.

CHAPTER 7

Responsibility/ Checking OCD

M any resources on the treatment of OCD will refer to "checking OCD" as a subtype of the disorder. This language is somewhat problematic, because checking is a compulsion, not an obsession. Checking is a behavioral response to a thought, feeling, or physical sensation that involves your heightened sense of responsibility. So the obsession is a fear of being irresponsible, and the compulsion is to check that no irresponsible action took place. The drive to check is a drive for certainty that something has not been left in such a state that it will cause a future catastrophe. This can be found in various obsessions, such as "just right OCD," harm OCD, or moral scrupulosity, but it can also be an issue of general-responsibility fears, which is why we are including it as a unique chapter.

Typically obsessions related to responsibility/checking OCD include:

- Fear that lockable items (doors, safes, and so on) have not been truly locked

- Fear that appliances have been left on (stoves, faucets, and so on)

- Fear that parking brakes or other safety measures have not been properly secured

- Fear that correspondence (e-mails, texts, letters, and so on) was improperly sent or contained the wrong information

What are some things you feel responsible for that trigger your urges to check?

_____

_____

_____

Typical compulsions for responsibility/checking OCD involve:

- Visual checking of items in a repeated or ritualistic manner (this may be paired with counting or vocal rituals)

- Tapping or repeated touching of items to ensure that they are locked or off

- Returning to check items after leaving in order to ensure that they are in the locked or off position

- Reassurance seeking from others that things have been properly checked

- Mental review of checking behaviors to gain a sense of certainty that they were appropriately checked

What are some compulsions that you act on to feel certain that you have responsibly checked something?

_____

_____

_____

_____

Acceptance Tools for Responsibility/ Checking OCD

At the core of all checking is the desire to rid yourself of the feeling that something is not as it should be. When a person without OCD locks a door, he generally walks away with the feeling that something has been accomplished. This is a chemical experience that occurs in the brain. The body's response to this change in brain chemistry is a sense that something has been "completed." The mind's response to this is a sense of ease and accomplishment, however small—a *letting go* of whatever was being attended to. If it's not the sense of "done," it's the sense of "good enough."

The OCD brain fails to release the chemicals effectively in this regard, so the body feels unease. The mind interprets this unease as *Something is wrong*. To use mindfulness skills here would be to observe that the mind is picking up this *Something is wrong* message, and not to intellectualize it into meaning that you have to go back and check.

Part of acceptance for this form of OCD includes accepting thoughts about the consequences of not checking. As you walk away from your front door, pull out of your driveway, and head down the street, you will be presented with thoughts about a variety of catastrophic events that could occur as a result of your failing to appropriately check. The faucet may malfunction as a result of being left running, which may cause the house to flood. A light left on may burst and cause a fire. The unlocked door may make your home just that much more sensitive to attack. If only you had checked, the home invasion wouldn't have occurred! Mindfulness asks that we let these movies play in the background of the mind, and commit to the decision not to do the compulsion. This means also accepting the presence of the worst kind of discomfort for an OCD sufferer, the sense of irresponsibility.

Practice: What thoughts, feelings, physical sensations, or other internal data do you believe you will need to mindfully accept in order to overcome your responsibility/ checking OCD?

_____

_____

Meditation Tips for Responsibility/ Checking OCD

For the "checker," meditation is really allowing the sensation that something has been left undone. It's the sensation of walking around with one shoe untied, while knowing that all you have to do is bend down and tie it, but you are resisting simply to combat the OCD. So as you anchor yourself to your breath in meditation, notice how the OCD pulls you aside to ask what was left on, what might start a fire, how someone might break into your home or get hurt through your negligence. Welcome these thoughts as passing strangers on a busy New York street—traffic, yes, but traffic you can glide through. Respond to an alert message like *Is it locked?* with thoughts like: *Okay, there are those locking thoughts I've been having. I'm breathing in and I'm breathing out, and I'm also noticing that there's this urge in me to go look again, to get certainty that I've checked the right number of times. I can feel it right here in my chest and in my forehead. Okay, I'm going to practice not minding that feeling for now. Maybe later I'll check, or maybe not. I'm going to focus my energy in this moment on this moment, which entails breathing in and breathing out. Checking urges can hang out in the back if they want. They will get attended to when I so choose.*

Assessment Tools for Responsibility/ Checking OCD

Catastrophizing plays the largest role in this form of OCD, because the checking urge is based largely on a desire to avoid catastrophic consequences. People with responsibility/ checking OCD live in a world not unlike the characters in the movie series *Final Destination*. In those films, death targets victims through a series of minor mishaps triggering one another in increasingly dangerous ways. So in the OCD mind, a parking brake checked only once, not twice, results in a malfunction that leads to the car rolling down the street, which leads to a car crash that leads to a fire that burns down a house and so on.

Discounting and minimizing play a large role here as well. After all, how many times have you burned down the house because you failed to check one more time? How many times did driving back home and making sure the garage door was completely flush with the ground really make a difference anywhere but in your feelings? So use experience-based logic when challenging checking thoughts. Remember, too, that emotional reasoning can confuse you into thinking that anxiety is evidence that something is left undone.

What cognitive distortions do you think play a key role in your responsibility/checking OCD?

_____

_____

_____

Overall, if you are suffering from this form of OCD, use assessment tools with caution. The tendency here is to quickly fall victim to mental review and self-reassurance: *Did I lock that? Yeah, I locked that. I locked that, right? I always lock that. Of course, I locked that.* That approach won't help, because it only sends the message back to the OCD mind that an investigation of your unease is warranted. So when you are doing cognitive restructuring for checking urges in particular, focus on the evidence, but also on acceptance of your lack of proof.

Practice: Keeping in mind that cognitive restructuring is about resisting the compulsion rather than proving the obsession wrong, try doing some automatic thought records on situations that come up for you. See the following sample record.

Sample Automatic Thought Record

| Trigger
What set you off? | Automatic Thought
What is the OCD saying? | Challenge
What is an alternative to the distorted thinking? |
|---|---|---|
| Thought about the stove while going to bed. | I probably thought about the stove because I left it on. I have to go downstairs and check to make sure it's off, or else the house may burn down while I sleep. | I don't know why the stove popped into my head, although the things I obsess about are likely to occur to me just before I prepare to go unconscious for the night! I don't know for sure that the stove is off, but in my experience, I have no reason to leave it on after cooking. I would prefer that no fire happened, but checking won't guarantee anything either. I'll have to take the risk that this is just a thought and lie here until I fall asleep. |

Action Tools for Responsibility/Checking OCD

Fortunately, with responsibility/checking OCD, the obsessions and compulsions are somewhat more concrete than in other obsessions. You are afraid that something bad will happen through negligence, and you have a compulsion to check. So start by making a list of all of the things that you check compulsively (see the following section). To determine the hierarchy, think about the level of discomfort you would feel if you chose to reduce or eliminate the checking of that item.

In Vivo ERP for Responsibility/Checking OCD

In many cases, you may find it easier to start by reducing or modifying the checking compulsion, rather than eliminating it from the beginning. If you customarily check the stove four times and verbally announce to yourself that the stove has been checked, look at the checking, the numbers, and the vocalizing as individual compulsions. Then you can practice checking the stove without vocalizing it or checking the stove three times before you move on to more challenging resistance.

With each change in your checking behavior, there will be OCD payback. It may come in the form of physical anxiety, powerful mental-review urges, or burdensome images of tragedies. This is where you need to let the mindfulness skills pick up the slack and allow for this experience to happen. When your OCD mind becomes witness to your ability to tolerate this discomfort, it begins to pull back on the checking urges. When this happens consistently, the brain itself begins to present the idea of checking as less important.

Here are the things that I typically feel the need to check, in order of importance to me:

_____

_____

_____

_____

_____

Imaginal Exposure for Responsibility/Checking OCD

Internally, you can do exposure with the fear of having been irresponsible, by using flooding techniques (see the section "Flooding in the Moment" in chapter 3). As you walk away from your checking urges, you'll notice thoughts about what could go wrong as a result of your not checking. Try agreeing with and embellishing those thoughts with things like, *Yep, gonna get a $50,000 water bill, because I didn't retighten the shower today,* or *Right now a group of thugs is rummaging through my underwear drawer, because I didn't properly lock the front door.* Be flippant with OCD instead of defensive. Headlines are a good technique to use here too:

"Neighborhood Mourns Loss of Local Church Ruined by Fire: Last Person to Leave Could Have Checked Outlets but Chose Not To."

You can practice your flooding skills daily by also doing imaginal exposure scripts. Here are some ideas to guide you through a script for responsibility/checking OCD:

What will I fail to check one day?

_____

_____

_____

_____

Where will I be when I find out that my failure to check resulted in a catastrophe?

_____

_____

_____

_____

What is the catastrophe (make it intense), *and how will my body react to the news?*

_____

_____

_____

_____

What will others think when they discover that the catastrophe could have been prevented?

_____

_____

_____

How will I cope with the awareness that my failure to check caused a tragedy and that I'll never forget this fact?

_____

_____

_____

What does this say about my level of competence and about me as a person overall?

_____

_____

_____

_____

How will my mental health deteriorate from this point, rendering me incapable of functioning?

_____

_____

_____

_____

CHAPTER 8

Just Right OCD

Too often OCD sufferers are mocked in the media as being "clean freaks" or organization nuts. While a healthy sense of humor about the lengths we go to in order to feel okay is probably warranted, it's important to remember that for you, the opposite of feeling *just right* about something is feeling dead *wrong* about *everything*.

Just right OCD (also known as *symmetry* OCD, *organizational* OCD, and *perfectionism* OCD) deals primarily with the obsessive fear that something is not precisely as it should be. While all forms of OCD involve strategies for feeling "right," identifying it here as its own form of OCD can be helpful, because triggers can vary so widely.

Typically triggers include:

- An awareness that an object or behavior is not symmetrical with another object or behavior

- A feeling of unease when completing a routine activity

- A concern that an item does not belong in a specific location

What are some things you think must be adjusted if they seem off to you?

_____

_____

_____

Typical compulsions typically involve:

- "Fixing" objects to look "right" in a given space (for example, straightening a picture frame or lining things up perfectly on a desk)

- Repeating a behavior that has been done on one side on the other side (for example, tapping your right leg after noticing that you've just tapped your left leg)

- Repeating a behavior to feel "right" (for example, repeating walking through a doorway or shutting a drawer)

- Checking to see if things appear as you feel they *should* (for example, reviewing the placement of two pillows on a bed to make sure they are in the perfect position)

What are some compulsions you do to make an "off" feeling "just right" again?

_____

_____

_____

_____

_____

Acceptance Tools for Just Right OCD

For someone suffering from this type of OCD, the feeling of being just slightly off is similar to the contamination OCD sufferer's feeling of having something disgusting on her hands. It's a significantly unpleasant feeling, and it coincides with a lot of catastrophic thoughts about being stuck that way forever.

You may have been told, "Just move on," "Let it go," or "Stop acting weird," receiving absolutely no sympathy for what that really means to you. In keeping with an earlier metaphor, it's the equivalent of asking someone to spend the rest of his life walking around with only one sideburn—seeing it in the mirror every day, being told it looks fine, and yet feeling absolutely certain that it must be changed.

This OCD fear is being informed primarily by an emotional state, a feeling that something is not the way it needs to be. Mindfulness in this situation means identifying that feeling and everything it encapsulates, including thoughts about being anxious, shame about not being able to just move on, and physical symptoms that range anywhere from basic anxiety to disgust. Once this experience is fully acknowledged, it then needs to be allowed to exist as another of life's experiences. The hardest part of acceptance in this form of OCD is knowing that the compulsion is often as simple as briefly touching something or moving something ever so slightly. It's the feeling of having relief just within reach but behaving as if it were actually out of reach. It's the image of a carrot on a stick wherein the stick is short enough to reach the carrot, but the carrot is there to be observed, not eaten.

To use mindfulness skills for this form of OCD, try to allow that "off" feeling to be exactly as it is. Find out where you feel it in your body: Your chest? Your shoulders? Breathe into it and carry it with you as if it belongs there. Carry it with you on your way to doing something greater than your compulsive fixing. Let the "off" feeling come along for the ride if it must, or let it fade away because you are too interested in attending to something else.

Practice: What thoughts, feelings, physical sensations, or other internal data do you believe you will need to mindfully accept while you treat your just right OCD?

_____

_____

Meditation Tips for Just Right OCD

If you choose to use daily meditation as part of your mindfulness training for this form of OCD, you will likely find that urges to fix things will vie for your attention during your meditative practice. Don't shun them. Smile on them. Tell yourself, _There are my urges to fix. Okay, I see them asking for my attention. They can join me as I meditate. I don't need to get rid of them. But I'll choose to turn from them and toward my breath for now. If they wish to breathe down my neck as I do so, I don't mind. Perhaps I'll attend to them after my meditation, perhaps not. For now, in and out._

Assessment Tools for Just Right OCD

Because so much of this obsession centers on ideas of right or wrong, on or off, straight or crooked, and so forth, once again we want to address all-or-nothing thinking in cognitive restructuring. Four pens lined up with the fifth just off to the side is not the absence of five perfectly lined pens. It's simply five pens, as they are.

Magnifying and catastrophizing play a large role here too, because you may be primarily concerned with the minor detail turning into a major problem that you can't stop dwelling on. Emotional reasoning plays a key role by pressuring you to assume that something needs to be fixed because it doesn't feel right.

What cognitive distortions do you think play a key role in your just right OCD?

_____

_____

_____

Practice: Try doing some automatic thought records on situations that come up for you that just don't feel *right*. See the following example.

Sample Automatic Thought Record

Trigger What set you off?	Automatic Thought What is the OCD saying?	Challenge What is an alternative to the distorted thinking?
Left pants leg brushed against door frame as I entered the room.	I have to reenter the room and make sure my right pants leg brushes against the door frame so that it's even.	This is a typical OCD challenge for me. If I sit with this feeling about asymmetry and resist my compulsion, it might eventually go away, saving me the embarrassing burden of having to repeat my steps. This feeling I'm having right now is to be experienced, not avoided.

Action Tools for Just Right OCD

Don't be discouraged if you have difficulty developing a graduated hierarchy for your OCD. Because the obsession largely centers on perceived perfection, seemingly small triggers may be as disturbing to you as more obviously upsetting triggers. The difference between something being slightly not right and completely wrong is often hard to distinguish and very often not worth the energy; plus, it could lead to compulsive mental review anyway. As a guide for how difficult each exposure might be, just try to use mindful awareness of your emotional state in the face of each trigger.

In Vivo ERP for Just Right OCD

Overall the objective should be to increase your awareness of the urge to "fix" and to choose to sit with the "off" feeling instead. However, walking away from a crooked pillow may be easier than walking away from a crooked parking job, so start by listing all of the things you have felt compelled to fix recently and seeing if they have varying degrees of intensity.

Here are the things that I typically need to make feel right, in order of importance to me:

_____

_____

_____

_____

You can do direct exposure by purposefully touching or engaging with objects on one side and then trying to generate an urge to touch them on the other side that will go unheeded. Another exposure technique is to intentionally make things *close to*, but just less than, perfect. You can practice general exposure by purposefully leaving things undone, such as leaving cupboard doors open slightly or leaving a book crooked on a bookshelf. The exposure goal here is to generate the "off" feeling, and practice being with it instead of fleeing from it. It may be difficult to predict how you will respond to each trigger and thus difficult to create an exposure hierarchy, so work off your list as best you can and try exposure in the moment, as the opportunity arises.

Practice: List ways in which you can generate the "off" feeling for exposure, and list typically "off" situations that you can use as exposure opportunities.

_____

_____

_____

Imaginal Exposure for Just Right OCD

Quite often the underlying fear for this form of OCD is grounded in the idea that the off feeling must go away, or it will cause intolerable consequences. You can use imaginal scripting to make contact with the fear of these consequences, and to help train you to stay in the ring with the off feeling. Use the following questions to help you generate an ERP script:

What is an example of something that makes me feel off?

_____

If I fail to fix it, how will I feel?

_____

If this feeling doesn't go away, how will it affect my behavior?

_____

What changes in my mood, attention, or behavior will others notice?

_____

How will my inability to stop feeling "off" or to stop thinking about the trigger ultimately keep me from functioning?

_____

What will the rest of my life look like if I'm unable to function?

_____

CHAPTER 9

Harm OCD

*H*arm OCD focuses on unwanted, intrusive thoughts of a violent or tragic nature. This may include fears related to your harming others or a fear of harming yourself.

Note that fear of self-harm is an entirely different phenomenon from actual self-harm behaviors (such as cutting). Similarly, fear of committing suicide is a different issue from suicidal ideation, wherein the obsessive fear of self-harm has to do with an unwanted intrusive thought of losing control; actual suicidal thinking has to do with the desire to end your life. Although OCD may interfere with your ability to feel certain about your intentions, if you believe that you have a genuine desire to harm yourself, it's important to seek immediate professional help.

Common obsessions in harm OCD include:

- [ ] Fear of suddenly snapping and violently attacking another person or yourself

- [ ] Fear of harming a dependent or loved one (for example, a parent fearing harming his newborn)

- [ ] Fear of failing to respond to violent thoughts appropriately

- [ ] Fear of having and acting out an uncontrollable urge to push someone into traffic, to jump out a window, or to follow some other impulse that would result in responsibility for a tragedy

- [ ] Fear of being overwhelmed by harm thoughts and choosing to act on them to relieve the pressure

☐ Fear of losing or having lost consciousness somehow and committing violent acts that you won't remember

☐ Fear of failing to wash or turn something off appropriately, and being responsible for a tragedy

☐ Fear of accidentally poisoning someone

☐ Fear of hitting someone with a car and not knowing it until the police track you down

☐ Fear of an inexplicable personality shift resulting in enjoyment of harm thoughts and acting them out

Check off any of the previous ideas that resonate with you, and in the following space, jot down any other harm-related ideas that concern you:

_____

_____

_____

Here are some compulsions typically related to harm OCD:

☐ Avoidance of people, items, places, or information (such as media) that trigger the unwanted harm thoughts

☐ Avoiding situations in which spontaneous acting out of harm thoughts would be possible (for example, giving a child a bath)

☐ Seeking reassurance that you did not or would not do a horrible thing

☐ Mentally reviewing thoughts and memories of events for the purpose of gaining certainty that you have not harmed or would not harm anyone

☐ Compulsive flooding: Trying to force yourself to imagine violent acts in an attempt to prove that you are disgusted by them and would not do them

☐ Thought neutralization: Purposefully forcing yourself to think a positive or otherwise contradictory thought in response to a harm thought

- [ ] Compulsive prayer or magical rituals: Repeating prayers or mantras by rote in response to unwanted thoughts

- [ ] Repeating behaviors in response to a thought of harming, in an attempt to complete them without having the thought

- [ ] Checking locations you've driven by to be certain you did not strike someone with your car, or looking back at people you've passed for signs that they have been harmed by you

- [ ] Researching violent offenders and comparing and contrasting them to yourself

Check off any of the previous compulsions that you are doing, and use the following space to add any others that might serve the same function:

_____

_____

_____

Acceptance Tools for Harm OCD

People harm one another. In this past year alone, we have seen harm OCD clients shaken by multiple, unrelated events involving a person walking into a presumably safe public place and murdering men, women, and children. Therefore it's not only normal, but also an essential part of being conscious, to have and be aware of violent, tragic thoughts. They are part of the human mind, whether we like it or not. Harm OCD sets in not because of the presence of harm thoughts, but because OCD demands that you be certain of why they are there. It doesn't feel as if it's enough to say, *They are there because I have a brain and am capable of thinking anything.* The OCD demands the impossible: a guarantee instead of an assumption.

These Are Normal Thoughts

How can a thought about hurting a loved one or killing yourself be called *normal*? To understand this, take a moment to consider what a thought really is. A thought is a mental event. It's a word that we use to describe a link between a chemical reaction in the brain and our awareness of it. A chemical event occurs, *something* happens, and then we become aware of that thing and call it a thought. The judgment of "normal versus abnormal" is used only to describe how the mind *interprets* that thought and what behaviors we choose to apply to it. The thought itself is nothing more than a word, a mental illustration, not an object or event, so how can it be anything but normal?

For mindfulness to be effective here, you must start from the perspective of accepting the presence of the harm thought. Accepting that the harm thought *happens* is not the same thing as accepting what the harm thought *implies* after you judge it. This is no easy feat. Frederick Aardema and Kieron O'Connor (2007) suggest that the degree to which you view yourself "as could be," versus viewing and trusting yourself "as is," plays a role in the intensity of this experience. While you view the harm thought you may be struggling with as unwanted, unreasonable, and contrary to your belief about who you are, it is undeniably coming from within and therefore is, in some way, your thought. Without your owning this reality, the OCD maintains a position of power over you.

> **Practice:** What thoughts, feelings, physical sensations, or other internal data do you believe you will need to mindfully accept as you alleviate your harm OCD?

_____

_____

_____

Meditation Tips for Harm OCD

Daily meditation, even if just for a minute or two, can be very helpful for developing mindfulness skills to alleviate harm OCD. As you sit and allow yourself to let the thoughts come and go, the OCD will very likely try to disrupt this process by flooding your mind with disturbing imagery. When you commit to accepting the presence of this imagery in your meditation, the OCD may respond by increasing the severity of the imagery. For example, you may mindfully acknowledge a thought of harming someone as just a thought; but then, as you return to your breath, the thought may appear as an image of a victim, or some other horror. Try your best to breathe through it. Imagine the presence of such thoughts as traveling through your breath. Rather than trying to make them go away, invite them to stay by not judging them: *Okay, so there's that image of violence. It is present in my head. Will I commit a horrible act? I need to make sure that's untrue, that it's not me. Okay, that's thinking. I can do thinking later. Right now I'm going to let myself attend to the in and out of my breath. If that thought wants to come along for the ride, it's most welcome. I don't need to do anything about it right now.* When you do this, you are likely to have feelings that you are used to avoiding, feelings of irresponsibility or shame. Give them the same treatment. Notice where they reside in your body. Imagine breathing into that part of the body, allowing space for the challenging feelings. Don't insist that meditation be pleasant. Insist that it be about *presence.*

Assessment Tools for Harm OCD

The nature of harm OCD is to assume that the thought represents an inherent warning sign about future violent events or serves as a reminder that past events must have been tragic. The greatest compulsive tendency here is to review the content of your character against the content of your thoughts in the hope that one will win out over the other. In other words, if you can convince yourself that you would never, or never did, harm anyone, you win the game. But the game is rigged. These things can't be proven. OCD uses cognitive distortions to trick the mind into hunting for a sense of certainty that can never be found.

As in every form of OCD, be on the lookout first for all-or-nothing thinking—for example, *Normal people never have violent thoughts.* Take the risk of reminding yourself that violent thoughts are indeed normal, and that merely *having* them is not important to review.

Harm OCD may have you living in constant fear of thoughts that "go bump" in your head. This feeling presents so close to guilt or madness that it seems to you as if you *must* have committed a crime or must be about to snap. It feels real. But feelings aren't facts, so pay attention to emotional reasoning when the OCD is saying, *I feel anxious when I have these thoughts, so they must mean that I'm about to act on them.*

If you struggle with harm OCD, you will also be zeroing in on all things harm related. The OCD may use violence in films, feelings of irritation about your being stuck in traffic, or even the positioning of your body as a way to try to connect things to your obsession, as in *I moved my hand in the direction of my child while having a harm thought, so I was very close to strangling her.*

Be aware of the tendency to compare yourself to people who frighten you (for example, famous serial killers). The OCD looks for ways to trap your mind into believing that *anything* you may have in common with *any* person who did something horrible makes *you* more likely to be horrible. This comparison distortion leads to a lot of compulsive review and avoidance that only strengthens the OCD.

What types of cognitive distortions show up the most with your harm OCD?

_____

_____

One of the things that makes harm OCD so frustrating is your awareness that your thoughts make no sense, and yet you feel helpless to do anything about them. It's as if you were screaming, *This isn't the truth!* but your mind is telling you in a low, booming, overpowering voice, *You know it is, because you are evil.* But the fact that the rational voice is buried in there somewhere means that you can access it and cultivate it without acting on compulsions, so that its volume can compete on its own with the OCD thoughts.

Practice: Try doing some automatic thought records on situations that trigger harm thoughts. See the following sample automatic thought record.

Sample Automatic Thought Record

Trigger What set you off?	Automatic Thought What is the OCD saying?	Challenge What is an alternative to the distorted thinking?
Using knife in the kitchen to prepare food.	I'm going to snap and cut someone with this knife. I need to ask someone else to cut these vegetables, because it isn't safe for me to be around knives.	Yes, this is a knife, and knives are used for cutting. Just because I am aware of this doesn't mean I'm going to cut someone. Not everything I am aware of is about my OCD. I have an urge to avoid it, because I don't like the way I feel right now. Getting someone else involved won't allow me to overcome this feeling.

In harm OCD, it's especially important to remember that objective thinking is not *positive* thinking. It's admitting what you don't know and being willing to function without certainty. Trying to prove that nothing bad will happen only ends up being another self-reassurance compulsion and another reason to engage in mental review. The key to cognitive restructuring for harm OCD always comes down to mindfully accepting that you don't know what thoughts mean, and that you also don't have enough evidence to assume that they mean something important.

Action Tools for Harm OCD

The exposure is only as good as the response prevention, so early exposure work needs to start at the level at which you feel capable of resisting compulsive responses. Don't be ashamed if this means that all you can do is read this chapter right now. The fact that you are reading it is exposure, and the fact that you are continuing is response prevention. You're already doing it.

In Vivo ERP for Harm OCD

As in contamination OCD, a good place to start would be to look at avoidance strategies that can be removed. For example, you may have taken all the knives out of the kitchen and put them out of reach, for fear that you might have a psychotic break and suddenly want to use the knives to hurt people. So start by placing the knives in the knife drawer, where they belong. Once that idea becomes tolerable again, exposures may involve using knives to cut food while you're alone, and then later doing so when other people are present (it may be the reverse if you have a fear of self-harm).

This early stage of ERP should also involve eliminating any seeking of online or vocalized reassurance. Family members caught up in the OCD should be educated to understand that these questions, annoying as they may be, are coming from a place of extreme pain and a desperate attempt to alleviate that pain. But along with this understanding must come a commitment to withhold reassurance, to remind the sufferer that loved ones won't participate in the compulsions.

Depending on the intensity of the symptoms, it may be useful to start with exposure to triggering words alone—for example, "kill," "murder," "hit-and-run," "manslaughter," "stab," "snap," "vicious," "cruel," "maniac," and so on. This may also involve words that remind you of harm triggers, like "girlfriend," "car," the name of a city, and so on.

Practice: If you feel ready to try this, using the following space, write a list of trigger words.

_____

_____

_____

_____

As you begin to feel prepared to confront a higher level of discomfort, exposure to watching the news or reading news articles about murder or other acts of violence can be helpful. The important thing here is to read the article about the person who "snapped," and to resist any compulsive urge to convince yourself that you are any different from that person. Exposing with the intention of proving that you are safe will always backfire. Choose to sit with and habituate to the discomfort, rather than compulsively reassure yourself. Start with the mindful perspective of _Yes, I am reading about a thing that happened to a person._ As you move up in the intensity of your exposure work, start agreeing with the OCD more directly: _Yep, that's me; I'm totally going to do that._

As with any exposure met with response prevention, the scary news story about the psycho killer eventually returns to its natural state: a story about a person who did a terrible thing. Until then, it will appear as an ominous warning of horrible crimes you have yet to commit. Remember that such appearances are mere thoughts and feelings, not threats and facts.

Ramping It Up

Higher levels of exposure may involve watching horror movies, serial-killer documentaries, and so on, particularly ones with story lines that resonate with your fear, again putting emphasis on resisting compulsive analysis or compulsive self-reassurance.

Use the following space to start constructing an exposure hierarchy for yourself. What things, people, or places do you avoid because of harm thoughts? What ways do you get reassurance about harm thoughts? What mental rituals can you work on labeling and rejecting?

_____

_____

_____

_____

_____

Imaginal ERP for Harm OCD

Because harm OCD so often involves mental review of thoughts and feelings that are unreasonable to re-create directly, imaginal exposure can be an important tool for approaching and conquering the obsession. If the idea seems totally out of the question today, don't judge yourself for not wanting to "go there" quite yet, but if you feel ready to try a harm script, try answering the following questions.

A good ERP script for harm OCD typically begins with a statement that you will snap under the pressure of the thoughts, that your "true identity as a killer" will be unleashed, and then this is followed by a play-by-play of the violent act. Don't pull any punches.

What will you do if your fears became reality?

_____

How will the other person or people involved react to what you've done?

_____

How will you feel when you become aware of what you've done? Will there be remorse and shock, or will you have become someone who enjoys it? How will you react to those feelings?

_____

_____

_____

What do your living loved ones think about you afterward? What does the world think about you?

_____

_____

How does your life ultimately end, and what legacy do you leave behind?

_____

_____

_____

If it's done right, a good exposure script gives you direct contact with the OCD. It demonstrates to the brain that you are capable of being face-to-face with a trigger while not doing compulsions. Eventually the exposure script returns the story to its natural place, just as other forms of ERP do: a bunch of words describing a thought—not a threat. Stay connected to the triggering thoughts during scripting, and try to intentionally maintain a level of discomfort that you can habituate to.

"What If It Turns Me Evil?

You may be concerned that these scripts might change you for the worse. This is a common fear in scripting for all forms of OCD. This idea of being changed by scripting (or any exposure) encapsulates the entire problem with the way your OCD has you viewing thoughts and feelings. To the harm OCD sufferer, violent thoughts are contaminants. To be with them means to be contaminated by their evil. Just as someone with contamination OCD may fear that contact with a public restroom will give him a terrible disease, the harm OCD sufferer fears that contact with harm thoughts will turn her into a monster. Exposure therapy is not just about proving this fallacy wrong. It's about redefining your relationship to thoughts and feelings altogether, letting go of trying to control the uncontrollable, and investing the saved energy in addressing the _controllable_, your actual present behavior.

It's Already Too Much

If you are struggling with harm OCD, then the idea of accepting the thoughts or doing exposure work may seem like too much to take on. You already may be spending the majority of your time counting down the minutes until the next time you can sleep so that you can get a break from thinking. Don't give up on yourself. Although it's true that exposure is hard work, you're probably not bad at hard work. You have to work hard every day to put on a face that looks "semi-sane" so that your loved ones and coworkers don't ask you a bunch of questions that you can't answer (like, "What's wrong?").

CHAPTER 10

Sexual Orientation OCD (HOCD)

The prevalence of sexual orientation obsessions is often underestimated. Monnica Williams and Samantha Farris (2011) found that 8 percent of OCD sufferers identified themselves as currently obsessing about sexual orientation, and 11.9 percent had symptoms at some point throughout their lifetimes. The problem is that people tend not to get treatment and to avoid talking about it, because so many people have such widely varying opinions about what it means to have different kinds of sexual thoughts.

Sexual orientation OCD is often referred to as *HOCD* ("H" standing for "homosexual") or *gay OCD*, although it's not exclusive to heterosexuals, and someone who identifies as homosexual can just as easily be plagued by obsessive fears of being straight. Sexual orientation OCD is the fear of not being certain about your orientation, paired with the fear of never being able to have a healthy, loving relationship with a partner to whom you feel genuinely attracted. The obsessive fear is rooted in the terror of living with uncertainty, not just being of one orientation or another.

Here are some common obsessions in HOCD:

- Fear that the presence of thoughts, feelings, or sensations contrary to your original orientation means that you are now defined by another orientation

- Fear of living "in denial" of your sexual orientation

- Fear that others see you as being of a different orientation

- Fear that life situations are indicators of orientation issues (for example, troubled relationships, tastes in music, changes in libido)

- Fear that past experiences prove that you are of a different orientation

- Fear that feelings for friends are indicators of sexual attraction

- Fear that recognizing attractive qualities in someone means that you are orientated toward that gender

What are some of the ways in which your HOCD presents itself?

_____

_____

_____

_____

_____

_____

Here are some common compulsions in HOCD:

- Mental review of life experiences aimed at proving or disproving orientation

- Reassurance seeking (including self-reassurance) that you are of your chosen orientation

- Avoidance of various triggers (for example, gay neighborhoods, gay media, clothing associated with feared orientation, and so on)

- Mentally or physically checking of the groin for evidence of stimulation in the presence of thoughts about a person of the same sex

- Compulsive use of orientation reminders (for example, watching straight pornography more than usual in an attempt to reassure yourself that you are straight)

What are some ways in which you attempt to feel certain that your HOCD fears are not true?

_____

_____

_____

_____

What Is Attraction?

"Attraction" is a word we use to describe the feeling of being pulled into something like a magnet. We generally conceptualize this feeling of being pulled in as evidence of our desire to be near someone or something. When we look at an attractive landscape in nature, we desire to be near it. When we see an attractive person, this also compels us to linger. It may be envy that draws us in, saying, for example, *I wish I had a body like that.* Often it's just giving a thumbs-up to the universe: *Good one, universe; you made an attractive person.* OCD promotes a false assumption that all attraction is *sexual* attraction. The disorder interferes with the mind's ability to allow the possibility of your being "attracted" to someone while *not* wanting to engage in sexual behavior with that person.

Acceptance Tools for HOCD

The very word "acceptance" can be a major trigger if you suffer from HOCD. Try to remember that *mindful* acceptance is not about buying into the content of whatever thought your mind happens to have picked up. It's not *I am what I fear because I fear it.* Mindful acceptance is about saying, *Hey, look at that: one of those thoughts.* If you have OCD, you're having thoughts about your obsession. If your obsession is with sexual orientation, then you're having thoughts about sexual orientation. The key is to choose to respond only to the extent that you acknowledge that the thought *happened.*

Your OCD says that you must not have thoughts about being of another orientation, but these thoughts exist. People who say they've never had them are lying, not because they are secretly gay, but because you have to have "gay" thoughts to even know what the word "gay" means. The difference is that someone without HOCD is not associating the presence of the thoughts with anything particularly meaningful or personal. So if something necessarily exists and you are trying to prevent it from existing, this is not going to work out well. If instead you can accept the reality that a variety of sexual thoughts occur as a function of having a brain and a mind, then you can train yourself to treat those thoughts with whatever significance that *you*, not your OCD, deem appropriate.

Uncertainty in Sexual Orientation

As in other OCD manifestations, the role of accepting and tolerating your discomfort with uncertainty cannot be overstated. Accepting that there is inherent uncertainty in all sexual orientations can be challenging in the presence of anxiety, particularly when your mind is stuck in analysis mode.

Mindfulness asks that you look at the fact that you are having thoughts, feelings, and physical sensations and that this experience is causing you discomfort. Your challenge is to acknowledge and accept the presence of this discomfort without intellectualizing it or trying to sort out what it means. Like any unwanted thought, it has the potential to mean something that frightens you. This potential is not the same thing as evidence.

HOCD wants you to fear the potential that you are not who you think you are. Fearing uncertainty only gives uncertainty power over you. This only leads to more compulsions and more obsessions. Accepting the experience of doubt in the moment that it presents itself, without trying to change it, will allow for the doubt to go *through* you instead of consuming you.

Practice: What thoughts, feelings, physical sensations, or other internal data do you believe you will need to mindfully accept as you alleviate your sexual orientation OCD?

_____

_____

_____

Meditation Tips for HOCD

If you choose to use daily meditation as part of your mindfulness training for HOCD, you may find the OCD pulling you away from the present to investigate and resolve unwanted sexual imagery, ambiguous "gay" feelings, and any sensations that may occur alongside them, particularly in the groin. Your OCD will tell you that the presence of any of these things is important and that to treat them as *unimportant* would be evidence of *denial*. As you pay attention to your breath, let yourself look away, just momentarily, to observe this process that takes place in the mind. Say internally, *I'm doing that thing: When a thought or feeling comes up, I label it as "gay," and then I want to figure it out. I'm going to take this opportunity to let go of the urge to figure it out and return to my breath. The urge is welcome to stay, but not to commandeer my meditation.* If you begin to feel "in denial," then incorporate that feeling into the meditation. Breathe into whatever it is that you have come to call "denial." Let it flow through your body without your compulsively addressing it. No problem solving equals no problems. When you get pulled away from the meditation to solve problems, simply notice this and take the opportunity to practice returning to the present.

Assessment Tools for HOCD

By spending mental energy trying to *prove* your sexual orientation, you are only contributing to the mind's misconception that the thought was important and that there is some reason to doubt your orientation. Don't get conned into an OCD contest you can never win.

HOCD will drive the mind toward black-and-white notions that *any* thought about a different orientation means that you must be oriented in that way. This type of OCD then adds catastrophizing distortions, such as *If I allow this thought to go without being analyzed, it will change my orientation, and that will be the end of my life as I know it.*

Disqualifying positive things will likely play a major role in your HOCD, with distorted beliefs like *Even though I've only ever been attracted to girls, my noticing the abs on the guy at the gym is different and means that now I'm a homosexual.* Confusing uncomfortable feelings with facts (emotional reasoning) may be behind thoughts like *I feel uncomfortable around my same-sex friend, so I must be gay* or *I don't feel sexual in the presence of my date right now, so that must mean I'm gay.*

Be conscious of mind-reading and personalizing that may take place with your HOCD, such as assuming that people are thinking about your orientation or are acting a certain way because of their beliefs about your orientation.

What cognitive distortions do you typically see compelling you to analyze or avoid HOCD triggers?

_____

_____

_____

Practice: Try doing some automatic thought records on situations that trigger HOCD thoughts. See the following sample automatic thought record.

Sample Automatic Thought Record

Trigger What set you off?	Automatic Thought What is the OCD saying?	Challenge What is an alternative to the distorted thinking?
Saw same-sex kiss in movie.	I felt weird when I saw that movie, and maybe that means I'm gay. I have to find out if this is normal, and I have to review my past to make sure I've never felt this before.	Sexual imagery causes sexual sensations. Reviewing my past will only make me obsess more. I have to accept whatever I felt without trying to be certain of what it means. I don't need to know if I'm gay or straight right now. I'm having an urge to try to know. What I need to do is eat this popcorn.

Action Tools for HOCD

You may feel concerned that ERP for sexual-orientation obsessions means engaging in homosexual behavior to overcome your fear of being gay. This is missing the point of exposure to a fear. The HOCD fear is not about having gay sex, but is instead about being stuck with thoughts, feelings, and physical sensations that you think don't belong and that you think have the power to ruin your life. It's about the fear that an internal experience means something that you don't want it to mean. So *testing* yourself by engaging in sexual contact outside of your historical sexual orientation as a means to overcome this fear will generally backfire. In other words, do what you *want*. If you want to engage in a sexual behavior that feels natural and pleasurable for you, then do so. But don't engage in behaviors that are designed only to obtain certainty in response to your OCD.

In Vivo ERP for HOCD

Exposure to thoughts of other sexuality and the fear that you are not who you thought you were can take many forms. Your OCD mind tells you that you must not think certain thoughts because they are dangerous to you. But your rational self has the power to stand up to this bully and burn out the OCD circuits when you intentionally expose yourself to unwanted thoughts about your sexual orientation. ERP can be divided into visual exposure and situational exposure.

Visual Exposure

Visual exposure would typically involve looking at images or videos of things that trigger the unwanted thoughts, while resisting mental rituals to explain or neutralize the thoughts. To do this effectively, you would start this form of exposure with something mildly triggering, such as a picture of an attractive same-sex celebrity. Once this no longer elicits a fear response, the exposure would be heightened to repeatedly looking at pictures of a more sexual nature and, if applicable, ultimately viewing explicit pornographic material multiple times. For the exposure to be effective, the viewing of the imagery must coincide with resistance to any urges to reassure yourself. If you feel that the imagery is pleasing, then *be pleased* even if this terrifies you.

List some ideas for visual exposure here:

_____

_____

_____

Situational Exposure

Situational exposure would typically involve, for example, visiting gay neighborhoods, bars, and nightclubs; listening to "gay" music; reading coming-out stories; wearing triggering clothing; spending time with gay acquaintances; and so on. Remember, the mindful objective here is to allow these environments to trigger your feared thoughts, feelings, or sensations, and to practice *leaning into* them instead of fleeing from them.

List some ideas for situational exposure here:

_____

_____

_____

Imaginal Exposure for HOCD

The objective of these exposures is to intentionally, but gradually, raise the anxiety caused by your unwanted thoughts, and to ultimately demonstrate to your brain that you can tolerate the presence of these thoughts. Conversely, compulsions teach the opposite: that you cannot tolerate discomfort.

If you feel ready to give scripting a shot, use the following questions to help guide your HOCD imaginal exposure. If you're not ready, work on your compulsion list and begin cutting out the things you avoid. Imaginal exposure can often be the most challenging exposure on your hierarchy, so don't pressure yourself to take on more than you feel capable of being mindful of.

What would it sound like if you agreed with the OCD thoughts and expressed a confession that you were of a different orientation than presumed?

_____

_____

Now that the feared thought is real, what will you do next? Whom will you tell first? How will you tell that person?

_____

_____

How do people react when you come out?

_____

_____

What steps do you take to pursue a sexual or romantic partner in this new life?

_____

_____

How do you meet your partner, and what are the steps leading up to sexual intimacy?

_____

_____

What do you do in your sexual experience, and how does it feel?

_____

_____

Afterward, what do you imagine your emotional world will be like? How does this affect your future behaviors?

_____

_____

What are the long-term consequences of your new lifestyle? Do you die happily of old age with your new partner? Or does a series of negative events consume you and result in your dying alone?

_____

_____

_____

_____

_____

Don't beat yourself up if merely reading the previous questions is exposure enough. Making direct contact with fear is no easy feat. ERP only works if you commit to resisting doing mental rituals, and instead mindfully accept without protest whatever thoughts and feelings the OCD may throw at you. In more intensive ERP, you are not only accepting the thoughts, but also actively agreeing with them, diving headfirst into the fear instead of tiptoeing around it. Any effort to analyze the exposure for evidence of your sexual orientation results in the mind confirming once again that your sexuality is up for debate. In other words, if you stop doing mental compulsions aimed at obtaining certainty about your sexual orientation, your mind will learn that it's not necessary to have that certainty.

CHAPTER 11

Pedophile OCD (POCD)

Combining the worst of harm OCD with the worst of sexual orientation OCD, obsessions about being a predator of children can be debilitating to every aspect of functioning. The thoughts are abhorrent to you, the physical sensations that coincide with them can make you wish you were never born to feel things, and the worst part is you can't tell anyone. Nobody but an OCD specialist who has treated this form of the disorder multiple times has any idea what you're talking about. You feel you can't tell your friends, loved ones, or anyone else that you're afraid you might secretly want to molest children (a secret so great that even you don't know it!) or that you have unwanted intrusive thoughts about molesting children (how can you prove to your confidant that these thoughts are unwanted?).

OCD is isolating enough; and to have the burden of the most disgusting thoughts aimed at the most vulnerable, innocent people is more than anyone should be asked to put up with. But OCD fears related to the concept of pedophilia are actually relatively common; and treatment, although as challenging as any OCD treatment, can put you back in control of the way you respond to your mind.

POCD obsessions typically involve these types of thoughts:

- Fear of snapping and becoming a pedophile

- Fear of touching a child inappropriately

- Fear of being in denial of pedophilic tendencies

- Fear that your own childhood trauma predetermined you to become a child abuser

- Fear of developing a desire to have sex with children because of your intrusive thoughts

- Fear of being identified by others as a pedophile

How does your POCD fear present itself?

_____

_____

_____

_____

POCD compulsions typically include:

- Avoiding all places where children are present (especially avoiding being alone with children)

- Avoiding any triggering media (children's clothing catalogs, news articles about pedophiles, and so on)

- Mentally reviewing all behavior that takes place around children

- Mentally reviewing past sexual experiences to reassure yourself in the face of POCD fears

- Mentally or physically checking for response in the groin when you are around children

- Analyzing the appropriateness of all thoughts related to sex or children

What are some compulsions that you engage in to feel certain that your POCD fears won't come true?

_____

_____

_____

Acceptance Tools for POCD

Remember that you cannot control what your brain offers up at any point and that your mind is simply a satellite receiving a signal (not a sign!). This is especially true when your brain is presenting you with images of what we typically refer to as "the unthinkable."

To employ mindfulness for any OCD, you have to remember that the issue of content is ultimately irrelevant. Thoughts happen. Children happen. Sex happens. Pedophilia exists. All of these truisms collide to produce thoughts that combine things we like with things we find horrifying. Mindfulness asks only that we be aware that this has happened in the mind, and not delve into hidden meanings, signs, threats, or other assumptions about what the mind happens to be receiving at any given time. As in other sexual and harm-related obsessions, the obsessive fear of being a pedophile presents itself as such an assault on your sensibility that the automatic urge to analyze, neutralize, and destroy the thought can be overwhelming.

The types of intrusive thoughts seen in POCD are actually normal events. The OCD makes them louder and brighter, not more meaningful. A person who sees a child in a bathing suit will think both *child* and *bathing suit*. The thought *bathing suit* may trigger the brain to upload thoughts like *bikini* or *beach*. *Bikini* or *beach* may trigger the brain to present thoughts like *sexy* or the *Sports Illustrated swimsuit issue*. If you are a POCD sufferer, you will equate the simultaneous presence of both *child* and *sexy* in the mind as the same thought. You will then assume that the thoughts are related directly and that you are experiencing a pedophilic thought. Horrified by this notion, you are likely to engage in some form of avoidance or resistance to the thought.

"I Have to Know How Pedophiles Think"

A common belief in this form of OCD is that you need to be certain how a "real" pedophile thinks in order to be certain that you are not that kind of person. Because these types of thoughts are so disturbing to the OCD sufferer and yet so typical (and for the same reason), you may often have an urge to investigate and study the history of pedophilia in an attempt to gain certainty that you are incapable of turning into someone who enjoys it. This is a major mindfulness challenge, because it assumes that absolute certainty is available through research. This research may take the form of online or academic research, or even just research of your own sexual history, digging for proof that you are safe from becoming the worst thing you can imagine. But it's an OCD trap. No amount of evidence demonstrating the obvious differences between a person who fears sexually harming children and a person who chooses to sexually harm children will satisfy POCD. Therefore, the awareness of being unsatisfied becomes the feared evidence of "latent pedophilia."

Noticing That You Noticed a Child

Often, noticing the developing body is the trigger. In other words, the trigger is the presence of *adult* characteristics, not child characteristics. OCD distorts the inevitable presence of sexual *thoughts* that coincide with the visual presence of sexually developed *bodies* to mean the *orientation* toward those unwanted thoughts. This gets misinterpreted in the mind as wishing to engage in sexual activities with people who are inappropriately young. So part of the mindfulness challenge in POCD is to be aware that the trigger may begin with a healthy, *normal* response to postpubescent markers (breasts, body shape, and so on), but this gets mutated into something sinister by the subsequent compulsive analysis from the OCD.

Mindful acceptance of an intrusive POCD thought means watching the thought, the discomfort it prompts, and any physical sensations that may come along with it simply go by. The thought must go by without labels, without judgment, and without footnotes (for example, *I know this is a bad thought, but I'm going to let it slide because of my OCD*). It's a fringe thought. It's precisely because of your blessing and curse of a wide mind satellite that the fringe picks up thoughts of sexual deviance and harm. Mindfulness for POCD is accepting openly what the mind is receiving and what the brain is presenting, without intending to shut it down. It's through this ironic acceptance of their presence that such thoughts diminish and slip away.

Practice: What thoughts, feelings, physical sensations, or other internal data do you believe you will need to mindfully accept as you alleviate your POCD?

_____

_____

_____

_____

Meditation Tips for POCD

If you choose to use daily meditation as part of your mindfulness training for POCD, be prepared to be alone with your thoughts. You will have thoughts about being something that offends you. You are going to have thoughts about victimizing people you care about. You'll have feelings of dread and physical sensations that frighten you. Be willing to be afraid, not because there's validity to the OCD thoughts, but because fear is a present experience. The whole point behind meditating is to practice allowing yourself to stay present with the experience you are having. It's not about fleeing from that experience toward one that you wish you were having instead. So when the POCD tries to pull you from your breath, respond with, _Okay, there they are, those thoughts. Maybe they're really important and I need to do something about them, maybe not. Right now I'm here to practice letting them be as they are. So, hey there, thoughts. Do what you like. But right now I'll return my attention to my breath. I am aware that I'm having the thoughts. In this moment, I will let myself feel whatever I'm being offered and choose to keep coming back to my inhaling and exhaling._

Assessment Tools for POCD

Like other forms of OCD, the black-and-white, all-or-nothing thinking is typically the worst offender: _If I have one disturbing thought about a child, notice that a child is posed in a way that would be sexy were it done by an adult, think one second about my hands being where they shouldn't be as I change a diaper, then I'm a monster._

Discounting and minimizing positive things is also a common distortion in POCD thinking. In the presence of a spike, your entire history of never having hurt anyone, of always finding the sexualization of children abhorrent, and of babysitting your nieces and nephews a thousand times over goes out the window. You had a thought, and in your OCD mind, that thought changed things forever.

Selective abstraction comes into play whenever a POCD sufferer is in the presence of children or anywhere related to children. A walk down the street near a school suddenly feels like a walk through a nightmare, because a child could appear at any moment and you could have a thought about that child.

What cognitive distortions do you think drive your POCD?

_____

_____

_____

Practice: Try doing some automatic thought records on situations that trigger your POCD thoughts. See the following sample automatic thought record.

Sample Automatic Thought Record

Trigger What set you off?	Automatic Thought What is the OCD saying?	Challenge What is an alternative to the distorted thinking?
Noticing nine-year-old dancing at birthday party.	My noticing how cute this kid was means I secretly wanted to kidnap and rape her.	I have a tendency to get triggered by "cuteness" and worry if that means something else. I don't know what I secretly want to do, obviously. I don't need to investigate brain secrets. What I need to do is enjoy this birthday cake. Noticing a thought and doing something absurd are unrelated issues. I'll have to sit with this discomfort for now, but the cake is still cake.

Overall, the thing to understand about cognitive restructuring for POCD is that all of the distortions require buying into assumptions about the workings of the brain and the mind that are fundamentally false. Restructuring those assumptions is always about coming back to mindfulness. The OCD wants you to avoid children, disprove absurdist thoughts about them, and punish yourself for being aware of thoughts that you believe should never occur. These are compulsions, and to resist compulsions, you will have to accept what the mind receives, not what you think it means.

Action Tools for POCD

For people who have POCD as the primary obsession, few are willing to get treatment, even when they know it's just OCD. The fear that a therapist will tell them that it's not OCD, that they need some sort of "aversion therapy" for being a pedophile, can be paralyzing. Furthermore, those who seek help from psychoanalytically trained therapists may hear a lot of unnecessarily triggering talk about repressed sexual feelings for children and process this as a need to come clean about their subconscious desire to do vile things to them.

In fact, we recommend that if you struggle with POCD, it may be best *not* to share your obsessive thoughts with anyone but an OCD specialist, because there's a genuine risk that an uneducated treatment provider practicing outside his or her scope will interpret the thoughts in much the same way that your OCD does and may even mistakenly file a report that could complicate matters. This is not because your thoughts are horrible and you need to hide them. This is because your disorder has a specific treatment, and engaging in treatment with someone who doesn't understand OCD is not in your best interest. For more information on accessing appropriate therapists for treating OCD, see chapter 17 of this book.

In Vivo ERP for POCD

There's often resistance to ERP treatment, because the compulsions make you feel safe and the word "exposure" makes you feel doomed. *Exposure to pedophilia? No thanks!* Of course, as with other forms of OCD, exposure to fear is not the same thing as exposure to danger.

ERP for POCD doesn't involve watching illegal child pornography or doing inappropriate things with kids. It involves increasing the tolerance of uncertainty caused by the

OCD, and decreasing the avoidant behaviors that separate you from the rest of your family or community. In vivo exposures may include the following:

- Reading articles about convicted child molesters while resisting reassuring yourself

- Going places where children may be present (parks, toy stores, and so on) and allowing triggering thoughts to go unneutralized

- Watching mainstream films with pedophile characters

- Browsing catalogs of children's clothes and resisting urges to respond compulsively to unwanted thoughts

- Volunteering to babysit a triggering relative

What triggering situations do you think you can confront in treating your POCD?

_____

_____

_____

_____

Nowhere in the process of ERP is there any need for actual sexual behavior and certainly any risk of harm to children. But when you do stop avoiding your triggers, you may feel that the very presence, lack of avoidance, or mindful acceptance of unwanted thoughts is dangerous enough. Remember that this is a *feeling*, and something that can be observed and allowed to pass through you without your acting on compulsions.

Flooding can often take an active role in the treatment of POCD. In short, this is where the concept of agreeing with the thoughts takes its most literal form. The OCD says, *You noticed that that kid had a pretty smile. You're a sick child predator.* You respond with, *Yep, ya got me. I'm gonna go buy a van and lure a bunch of kids into it right after lunch.* If you use this technique, be aware of the risk that it will become a compulsion of its own. Use it as needed. Take another look at the "Flooding in the Moment" section in chapter 3 and how it differs from the compulsive flooding discussed in chapter 4.

Imaginal ERP for POCD

Imaginal exposure for POCD is extremely helpful and generally an essential part of treatment for obvious reasons (just as in harm OCD and HOCD). Often there's resistance to writing scripts about sexual molestation for the following reasons:

- *It's too horrible to put into words.*

- *Someone may find it one day and use it against me.*

- *If I write it, that makes it more real.*

- *If I write it, I might enjoy it, and that will prove my fear.*

What concerns might you have about writing imaginal exposure scripts for this obsessive fear?

_____

Working with a trained OCD specialist may be the key to your developing the capacity to approach imaginal exposure work for POCD. But if you will be using imaginal ERP on your own, be sure to educate yourself as much as possible beforehand by reviewing the concepts in this book and reading about POCD treatment in other books (see our book recommendations in the resources section).

Once prepared and educated on the process, you can do ERP to imagine the mind of the monster as if the monster were you, describing in detail how you would act out your obsession on an innocent victim, how that person would respond, what you would do afterward, and what life would really look like with the "Scarlet P." Use the following questions as a guide:

If your fear were true, how would you act on it?

_____

_____

What would your victim think and feel?

_____

_____

How would you respond to your victim after the act?

_____

_____

Would you get caught, and if so, how? Would you get away with it, and if so, how?

_____

_____

What would you think, feel, and do with the knowledge that you committed this act?

_____

_____

How would your loved ones respond to your behavior?

_____

_____

How would you live out the rest of your days?

_____

_____

_____

_____

Mindfulness is an essential tool for coping with the imaginal scripting experience. To let yourself come back from the horror of the POCD script with self-kindness is hard work. But like any obsession, habituation to fear is accomplished through repetition of exposure and resistance to compulsions. Without the fear response to the thoughts, those thoughts go back to their natural place in the universe, as nonevents in the brain picked up at the fringe of the mind, unworthy of special attention.

CHAPTER 12

Relationship OCD (ROCD)

OCD likes to go after big targets, whatever matters most to you. This could be your sense of morality, your sexuality, your kids, or your health. And, for many of us, our relationships hold such a high value in our lives that OCD can't keep its hands off them. *Relationship OCD (ROCD)* is difficulty in tolerating uncertainty about the quality of a relationship and the genuineness of your feelings about another person. This isn't the typical doubt you might expect when, say, one person is ready for marriage and the other isn't. This is the kind of doubt that seeps in insidiously and chips away at the very concept of love and fidelity. If you suffer from ROCD, you feel as if you are in a double bind, where your primary source of comfort and security in the world (your partner) becomes your primary source of anxiety. The OCD says that if you don't follow its arbitrary and impossible-to-satisfy rules, the relationship falls apart, and not only that, it's your fault—and not only that, the person you love most in this world suffers more than you do.

Obsessive fears in ROCD typically include:

- *What if I don't really love my significant other?*

- *What if the relationship is going to fail and I need to get out now?*

- *What if my partner doesn't know enough about me to make an informed decision about being with me?*

- *What if I would be a better match with someone else?*

- *What if I can't stop thinking about things that trigger me about my partner* (for example, a physical attribute, the person's sexual past, philosophical differences)?

- *What if I am not as attracted to my partner as I should be?*

What types of thoughts and feelings does your ROCD present you with?

_____

_____

_____

Typical compulsions in ROCD include:

- Mental review of everything pertaining to the relationship

- Compulsive confessing of doubts about the relationship

- Seeking reassurance about the relationship

- Mental checking of emotions associated with the relationship

- Scenario bending or theorizing about alternatives to the relationship as it is

- Avoidance of situations that trigger relationship obsessions (for example, trying not to notice attractive people, avoiding participating in discussions about sex or relationships, avoiding being alone with triggering people)

What types of compulsions do you engage in to get a sense of certainty about your relationship?

_____

_____

_____

"You're My One in a Million"

As with any OCD issue, the truth is that your worst fears *could* be true but obviously are *not*. Probably—that is, it cannot be proven with 100 percent certainty that your fears are basic nonsense, but the evidence supporting their *being* nonsense is readily available. Yet relationships seem to demand acceptance of particularly high levels of uncertainty. Your partner may be gone tomorrow. You may choose to go tomorrow. There very well may be someone out there who's a better match, presuming there's a clear definition of "better" and "match" for you to work with.

If your partner is one in a million, congratulations! That means that on a planet of seven billion people, there are seven thousand potential life mates who would make you very happy indeed. So what do you make of this? Nothing. You go on with your life, happily connected to someone you cannot prove is *the one*, calling that person "the one," feeling him or her as "the one," and letting go of the need for absolute certainty. Just as your hands are "clean" after a good wash, you are still not absolutely *certain* they are clean, and con-tamination OCD aside, you're okay with that.

Acceptance Tools for ROCD

Relationships are to be *experienced*, not calculated. OCD will use the argument that without proof, there's no love, and without love, there's no relationship. This is just another of the disorder's tricks designed to get you to act on compulsions. Acceptance of relationship fears doesn't mean that you should accept abuse or force yourself to stay with a person you despise. To accept intrusive thoughts about your partner and the legitimacy of your rela-tionship is to accept that part of the experience of connecting your life with that of another person *necessarily involves discomfort*.

Remaining steadfast in the not-knowing stance is quite challenging, especially when the OCD is bullying you to investigate, analyze, figure out what you need to do, and make sure it gets done now before catastrophe occurs. Without OCD, people doubt, fight, worry, and sometimes choose to go separate ways. OCD demands the impossible by asking you to decide *right now* what to do, while *blocking* you from staying present with what's happening in your relationship long enough to have any sense of what *to* do! In that state of urgent uncertainty, you are a slave to the OCD, and will do compulsion after compulsion to attempt escape.

Making matters worse, another human being is directly involved. There's a sense of responsibility for how the other person's life turns out. The fear that you stayed with the wrong person not only makes you hate what you've allowed yourself to become, but also makes you feel fully responsible for the choice your partner made to be with you.

As in other forms of OCD that don't display a high frequency of physical compulsions, mindfulness skills are an important part of separating the presence of the unwanted thought from the urge to review or seek reassurance. Part of mindful acceptance for ROCD is sitting with the discomfort that your partner and others may perceive you as being something quite different from what you are. For example, you may obsess about the image of your partner with his or her ex, thereby appearing to others to be a jealous person. But it's not the feeling of jealousy that drives your constant need for reassurance and mental review. It's the feeling that something is off that could somehow be made *right* if only you could get that last compulsion satisfied! It just *looks* like jealousy on the outside.

Similarly a person with obsessional fears that a relationship won't last may appear to others to be seeking a way out of that relationship. To the contrary, the incessant mental review of the situation is designed to generate a feeling that will allow you to stay *with* the person you love! So the mindfulness challenge here is not only to view your own thoughts and feelings as simply passing by, but also accept the thoughts and feelings you may have about being misunderstood by others.

Genuine Love vs. Checked Love

One of the most common mindfulness challenges in ROCD stems from the intrusive question, *Do I love my partner?* A classic example for the ROCD sufferer might be a man who sees his wife walk by and becomes aware of the thought, *She is so beautiful. I'm a lucky guy. I love my wife.* Then the OCD responds with, *Is that really love? Are you sure?* Taking the bait, the man might start purposefully thinking about the meaning of "love" and digging deeply into his mind to see if he can generate a *feeling* of love. He can. But because this feeling is generated by checking, or by force, what he ends up with in his mind is a synthetic version of the feeling of love. It looks like love, but it falls just short of seeming authentic. *See? Things are not as they seem,* says the OCD. The man may begin to notice his anxiety rising and dig again to see if he genuinely, truly, *really* loves his wife, or has just been conning himself to believe so all these years. He digs it up again, but just ends up with another hologram, a synthetic version of the synthetic version of his true deep feelings! It's a nightmare! He begins to overattend to the gap between the "real" love he felt when he first fell for his wife and the "synthetic" feeling of love he is conjuring up in his mind. The gap widens and becomes the most important idea to respond to anytime it's present in the mind. And it's present at all times! The OCD is now his master.

The lesson learned from this story is that you cannot have a genuine emotional experience while checking for a genuine emotional experience. This is also why you can't tickle yourself—you know you're doing it! Mindfulness for ROCD means letting go of the authenticating urges and accepting feelings of love as they are, unchallenged. The same goes for feelings of confusion and doubt about love. The goal is to allow yourself to experience these feelings, not to make sure they are fitting into the boxes where you think they should go.

Practice: What thoughts, feelings, physical sensations, or other internal data do you believe you will need to mindfully accept as you alleviate your relationship OCD?

_____

_____

_____

Meditation Tips for ROCD

If you choose to use daily meditation as part of your mindfulness training for ROCD, remember that meditation practice is not about trying to make sense of your relationship. To the contrary, what you want to practice in meditation is coexistence with things not making sense. The OCD drives you to treat every doubtful thought or feeling about your relationship as if it must urgently be resolved before everything falls apart. Meditation, as a practice of mindfulness, is about letting yourself sit and watch things fall apart. Let your thoughts and feelings crash into one another and create explosions in your mind. Notice them. Do not ignore them. But resist the urge to analyze or sort them out. Simply glance at them as they happen, and then return to your meditation. *I may be doing this whole meditation thing to make it okay that I don't feel in love. Wait. That's thinking. I don't need to do that right now. I'm breathing in, and I'm breathing out. There are thoughts about my relationship happening. That's fine. I don't mind. They can happen while I let myself stay here with my inhaling and exhaling. Maybe later I'll go back to all the mental review. That might be just fine. But in this moment, I'm going to practice staying here.*

Assessment Tools for ROCD

You may find yourself noticing that when things are great, they're great. But when your OCD is running the show, everything feels as if it's about to crumble. You're about to leave your partner, or your partner is about to leave you. Or worse, you're doomed to an eternity together in which you are smothered with regret and doubt. Watch out for these distortions in particular:

- **All-or-nothing:** *I must always feel 100 percent in love with my partner, or else we're wrong for each other.* The reason this is a complete OCD setup is that no one is capable of doing this. Feelings aren't set in stone for all time. They are fluid. They evolve, expand, shrink, and shift constantly, as they are supposed to.

- **Catastrophizing:** *If I don't know for certain that I'm with the right person, my life and my partner's life will be ruined.* Here again, you need to remember that the end or changing of a relationship isn't the end of the world, even if it's the biggest fear your mind is presented with. So not only is the future of a relationship unpredictable, but the worst predictions would be experienced in ways that are unknown.

- **Selective abstraction:** *I can't look at that mole forever!* Mindfulness, like love itself, is about taking in the bigger picture of yourself, not picking at the details. When you fall into a *romance*, you actively ignore the negative details that may be thrown at you. When you actually fall in *love*, you begin to see those negative details, but they are no longer negatives. You love these details for being a part of the person you love.

- **Mind reading and personalizing:** *She doesn't think I'm smart. She didn't respond to my text message, because she knows our relationship is a sham.* Here you fall for the trap of assuming that others' thoughts are accessible and knowable, and that others' behavior has intrinsic meaning. Neither of these things is true.

- **Hyperresponsibility:** *I have to tell my partner that I would have considered cheating on him if the opportunity presented itself, even if I can't prove this. I have to do this, because if I don't, he will spend the rest of his life married to a person who may not be worthy of his love, and I'll be responsible for his wasting his chance to be with the right person.* As in other forms of hyperresponsible thinking, the OCD makes it look as if you are charged with the task of ensuring that your partner makes the right choices in life, which isn't something you can control.

What types of cognitive distortions are at play in your ROCD?

_____

_____

Practice: Try doing some automatic thought records on situations that trigger your ROCD thoughts. See the following sample automatic thought record.

Sample Automatic Thought Record

Trigger What set you off?	Automatic Thought What is the OCD saying?	Challenge What is an alternative to the distorted thinking?
Noticing attractive person at work.	I must know for sure that this person is less attractive to me than my partner is. If I think this person is attractive, I have to tell my partner that I thought this.	Engaging in mental rituals won't give me any useful information and will only promote more obsessing. If this person has features I admire, that's fine, and I don't know what it says about my feelings for my partner. Compulsively confessing my thoughts to my partner is just my way of trying to avoid feeling discomfort. It always comes back to bite us both in the end, and I'm better off using my mindfulness skills on this one.

Action Tools for ROCD

The most common compulsions in this form of OCD are various forms of mental review, reassurance seeking, and confessing. As discussed with other obsessions, mindfulness here is often a major exposure in and of itself. When the thought about the relationship presents itself, it coincides with fearful feelings and, often, uncomfortable physical sensations. The urge to mentally review the relationship, figure out why everything is wrong or everything is okay, and lock down the feeling of safety can be overwhelming.

Mindfulness asks that you observe these thoughts, feelings, and physical sensations exactly as they are, and not engage in behavioral responses to change them. They are going *through* you. The exposure, then, is to allow the thoughts, feelings, and sensations to go unchecked and unreviewed as they pass by. Take the risk that your internal process represents your worst fear, and that you are realizing that fear by allowing the internal data to slip past you. Sit with the feeling that it's slipping by.

Catch yourself reviewing the relationship and label it as a compulsive behavior. It may feel like an automatic inevitability, but actively participating in it is always a voluntary behavioral choice. Let it go on in the background, but don't be the director of that movie. Be your own director. Once you've labeled the compulsive mental review, you can begin to disengage from it and return to the present. The present may be something unrelated, like work or a book. But the present may also be the feelings themselves. Observe the feelings; don't analyze them.

Reassurance seeking can be very difficult to resist. Don't feel ashamed if you believe that resisting reassurance seeking in the face of a relationship obsession is impossible. Many people suffering with ROCD feel that they simply cannot make it without at least one acknowledgment from their partners that everything will be okay. If your partner is on board with treatment and willing to see the difference between you and your OCD, then enlist his or her help with resisting reassurance. Take another look at the "Reassurance Seeking" section in chapter 4 for tips on how to do this.

Explaining ROCD to Your Partner

When you team up with your partner to fight the OCD, it's important that your partner understands some of what you are going through. If your partner doesn't have OCD, it may be a struggle for him or her to understand all of it, but if the person is willing to consider a basic sense of it, progress is much more likely. Let your partner know that the obsession is not really about him or her in particular. It's an obsession with disproving the OCD's distorted version of the relationship. Although the words your mind is grappling with may sound like *I'm afraid I don't love you,* it might be best to frame it as *I get stuck on details that get bigger and bigger in my mind, and the more I try to analyze it, the more my OCD gets the better of me. I need your help to block me from seeking reassurance until I come down from the obsessing. In the meantime, don't take anything I say about us too seriously.*

In Vivo ERP for ROCD

If you find yourself avoiding things that remind you of your relationship fears, then exposure strategies that focus on these things would be helpful. It's important to always stick to the plan of exposure *with* response prevention. Stay in contact with the thing that causes you discomfort, but mindfully accept the thoughts and feelings that get triggered. Don't tell yourself over and over that it's okay. Don't tell yourself anything. Have the thoughts and feelings without trying to neutralize them. The key here is to encounter your fear *without* mental reviewing or acting on other compulsions. Here are some examples of activities that might be effective exposures for ROCD sufferers:

- Watching triggering movies or listening to triggering songs

- Looking at pictures that remind you of the triggering obsession (these are good for general exposures too; see the "General Exposures" section in chapter 3)

- Visiting places that trigger the relationship obsession

- Resisting the urge to abandon or manipulate conversations that are heading into uncomfortable territory

- Resisting the urge to avoid being alone with a triggering person (for example, riding in the elevator with an attractive coworker)

- Resisting the urge to seek reassurance or confess triggering thoughts to your partner

What are some in vivo exposures you can start doing to make contact with your ROCD fears?

_____

_____

_____

_____

Imaginal Exposure for ROCD

The imaginal script for ROCD should focus on the idea that you have failed to see certain signs, and that the relationship is doomed to fail, you are doomed to hurt your partner emotionally beyond repair, or you are doomed to remain in the relationship unhappily obsessing about it until death or divorce. The script should include frank statements about things that your OCD has been telling you are wrong with your partner and the relationship, cruel admissions about attraction to other people, and sinister negative fantasies about each of your lives being ruined by your failure to act immediately on your thoughts and feelings. If you feel ready to use this technique, use the following questions as an outline for your script:

Why is this relationship doomed?

_____

_____

Now that you've admitted it, what will you do about it?

_____

_____

How will your partner be affected by this choice?

_____

_____

How will you respond to this?

_____

_____

If you break up, what will your life look like moving forward? If you stay together, how will the relationship be intolerable to you?

_____

_____

What will others think about the relationship choices you made?

_____

_____

What will you think or feel upon reflection of these choices in your old age?

_____

_____

If you don't feel ready to script out your fears quite yet, that's fine. Start exposure by eliminating reassurance seeking and avoiding confessing behaviors. Work on identifying and coexisting with the discomfort that your ROCD brings. Pay attention to the way you shift your attention when the discomfort is present. Bring yourself back to the present as best you can, and start moving in the direction of your discomfort one step at a time.

CHAPTER 13

Scrupulosity OCD

Scrupulosity OCD targets people who place a high value on philosophy, religion, life rules or laws, and existential meaning. It's often referred to as *religious OCD*, but it can follow the same trajectory for nonreligious moral concepts. People with religious scrupulosity focus primarily on the idea that they are failing to adhere to the rules or intents of their subscribed religions. People with moral scrupulosity focus primarily on black-and-white concepts of absolute rightness or wrongness in their behaviors and thoughts, independently of whatever religion they subscribe to.

Religious Scrupulosity

Joseph W. Ciarrocchi (1995) describes religious scrupulosity and its treatment with cognitive behavioral therapy extremely well in his book *The Doubting Disease*. He points out that the term "scruples" comes from the Latin word *scrupulum*, which means a small, sharp stone. Living with scrupulosity OCD is very much like trying to travel a great distance knowing that there's a stone in your shoe, but failing to completely get rid of it. As in other forms of OCD, it's this pervasive *feeling* that something is not the way it's *supposed* to be that drives compulsive behaviors.

Here are some common obsessions in religious scrupulosity:

- *I'm interpreting the scripture of my religious book incorrectly.*

- *I will be judged cosmically because of my failure to adhere perfectly to my religion.*

- *My thoughts about my religious icon or its opposite are inappropriate.*

- *The presence of certain events, words, or numbers is a sign of condemnation.*

- *I don't feel the right amount of faith.*

What types of intrusive thoughts or experiences do you have as part of your religious scrupulosity?

_____

_____

_____

Some common compulsions in religious scrupulosity are:

- Repetitive or rigid and ritualized prayer

- Reassurance seeking regarding religious concepts

- Thought neutralization: replacing antireligious thoughts with proreligious thoughts

- Mental review of religious thoughts, or mental checking of feelings about religion

- Exaggerated religious practice (for example, donating excessively in response to scripture about generosity)

- Avoiding people, places, images, or media associated with other religions

- Overattending to or avoiding numbers or symbols related to your obsession (666 is a common one, as are crucifixes, Magen Davids, and so on)

What types of compulsions do you engage in to feel certain that your religious scrupulosity fears won't come true?

_____

_____

_____

Understanding religious scrupulosity means first understanding that religion necessarily involves rituals. Rituals are designed to connect with your faith. When groups of people agree to engage in the same rituals, they connect with one another in their faith. Rituals in this context are good things. But they should be bringing you *closer* to your faith. When OCD targets faith, it can take those rituals and turn them into rigid compulsions that have little to do with connecting, and more to do with relieving discomfort.

The trap is that the more you try to obey the OCD (which presents itself *as* your faith), the more disconnected you will feel *from* that faith. Treatment for religious scrupulosity typically involves some amount of communication between your OCD therapist and your spiritual advisor. No therapist should be in the position of trying to get you to violate your religious rules. The therapist's job is to help you separate the OCD from the religion, so that the only thing being treated is the mental health challenge, not the faith.

You may feel very much afraid that exposure therapy will pull you away from your faith. This is the same state of mind that makes people with other obsessions fear treatment (*Exposure therapy to contaminants will make me sick or irresponsible, Exposure to sexual obsessions will make them define me*, and so on). To the contrary, your connection to your faith is being disrupted by the OCD, and freedom from your OCD will most likely result in a stronger, healthier commitment to your faith.

Moral Scrupulosity

Whereas religious scrupulosity may focus primarily on a fear of punishment by a higher power, moral scrupulosity focuses on a fear of guilt or punishment from society. It's an obsession with what legacy you leave behind, a good one or a bad one.

Common obsessions in moral scrupulosity are:

- *I am an inherently bad person.*

- *I must say yes to all requests.*

- *I must avoid all potential of selfishness.*

- *I must never offend anyone.*

- *I must know for certain whether all of my actions are right or ethical.*

- *I must never use a product that anyone could view as inappropriate* (for example, clothing that might be made in a country with unfair labor practices, pornography, alcohol).

- *I must be certain that I never waste a resource that's limited* (for example, water, electricity, gas).

What types of fears does your moral scrupulosity present?

_____

_____

_____

Common compulsions in moral scrupulosity are:

- Excessive mental review of *all* behavior for evidence of immorality

- Theorizing (*What would I have done in a hypothetical moral test?*)

- Confessing that something may not have been 100 percent moral

- Avoiding using products that have become associated with moral obsessions

- Seeking reassurance that you are a moral person

- Punishing yourself (being overly self-critical in response to a feared transgression)

- Checking excessively to ensure that a product is safe or a resource isn't being wasted

What compulsions are at play in your moral scrupulosity OCD?

_____

_____

_____

_____

Acceptance Tools for Scrupulosity OCD

The primary issue here is allowing the OCD to bully you into overanalyzing your relationship to your belief system. Mindfulness for scrupulosity involves accepting the philosophical process as it is and the related thoughts and feelings as they are, without investigation or judgment. Many religions promote the idea of not judging others, yet it's often open season on *yourself* when you have scrupulosity OCD!

As with other obsessions, you have to start with the assumption that the content of your thoughts has the potential to be true. *Potential* is not conclusive. It's the *opposite* of conclusive. But without accepting the potential, there's no way to mindfully observe the thoughts, feelings, and sensations without automatically judging their content as unacceptable. If you subscribe to a religious faith that promotes the idea that thoughts can and should be controlled, or that the presence of thoughts is the same as committing a behavioral act, you may struggle with reconciling MBCBT with your faith. Here is an area again where it may be helpful to communicate with a spiritual advisor and an OCD specialist together to find a pathway that will enable you to move forward with treating the OCD without challenging your religion.

For religious scrupulosity, you may be able to use your faith to aid in mindfulness. Intrusive thoughts may be viewed initially as threats but can be reframed as opportunities to *practice* faith. Allowing a thought that contradicts your religion to pass through your mind without judgment can be a great test of your commitment to your faith. While you may fear that letting such a thought come and go is the same as believing the content of the thought, you could instead view this as an offering from your higher power to practice nonjudgment, and to let go of the need for certainty above all else.

Subscribers to some religions may initially be concerned about mindfulness because of its association with Buddhist principles. But it's important to remember that no religion has ownership of the basic concept behind mindfulness, that you are not the same as what you see inside, and that you have the ability to observe your internal process.

With moral scrupulosity, mindfulness means observing the idea that you've done something wrong and, as with religious scrupulosity, using your belief in nonjudgment to guide your own nonjudgment of yourself. Notice the thought about wrongdoing. Watch it pass through you, unencumbered by ritualized responses. Breathe through the thought as it passes by and then, above all, come back. Return to the present. Return to this book, or whatever you were doing before you became aware that you might not be perfect.

What thoughts, feelings, physical sensations, or other internal data do you believe you will need to mindfully accept as you alleviate your scrupulosity OCD?

_____

_____

_____

Meditation Tips for Scrupulosity OCD

If you choose to use daily meditation as part of your mindfulness training for scrupulosity OCD, you are likely to find yourself acutely aware of the experience of being *wrong*. You are going to have the wrong thoughts, the wrong feelings, and the wrong physical sensations, and they will all seem to collude to make you feel unworthy of self-love, unworthy of a connection with your higher power, or unworthy of acceptance in society. As you pay attention to your in-breath and out-breath, to your body, and to that which is present, let yourself include this feeling of being wrong. Observe how your mind takes the signal from your OCD, and immediately makes attempts to unravel the wrongness and flee from discomfort. Observe and acknowledge, and then return to the present: *I am aware of thoughts about being a bad person and feelings of judgment from within and without. I can accept them as they are for now: thoughts and feelings. I can accept the discomfort I have when I turn away and return to my breath. If these thoughts and feelings want to join my breath, I won't resist them, but I won't engage them either.*

Assessment Tools for Scrupulosity OCD

Watch for all-or-nothing thinking first. *If I think one antireligious or immoral thought, then I am cut off from my higher power, eternally damned, or permanently labeled as a bad person.* We don't hold others to this standard. We forgive minor transgressions (major ones for people we love), and we also acknowledge that there is, in fact, a gray area in morality and faith. It's exactly that gray area that makes up the concept of faith. One cannot have faith while demanding proof. Faith is that which connects the gap between what's obvious and what we believe to be true.

Catastrophizing in scrupulosity focuses on the assumption that intolerable punishment is the only possible result of a failure to do compulsions or achieve perfection. In religious scrupulosity, the punishment is often eternal damnation. We won't attempt to define this concept here, because it's best understood through your own philosophical experience. However, what remains for challenge is the assumption that your punishment is coming based only on the *thoughts* of what you may have done, and the *feeling* that it was wrong. In moral scrupulosity, the catastrophic assumption is that society—or worse, *you*—will forever mark you as "bad." Even though there's no way to prove otherwise, the OCD will drive you to view the assumption as fact, rather than mindfully observe the assumption as, well, an assumption.

By definition, with scruples being small things, concern with them involves magnification. Failing to recycle a soda can gets distorted in the OCD mind as failing to be a decent human being. Mindfulness asks that we look at minor transgressions in our philosophical systems as being just that: minor transgressions. View them as they are, not just as they appear to be in the mind. Perhaps they mean important things, but assuming this only out of fear plays directly into the OCD.

Because guilty feelings can be so painful in scrupulosity OCD, emotional reasoning is an important distortion to look out for. The presence of guilt is not evidence of the commission of a crime. The investigation of that crime is then a compulsive ritual, a behavior that you engage in without evidence that this behavior must be done. *Feeling* wrong and *being* wrong aren't the same thing. Sitting with uncertainty about this gap between what you are feeling and what you believe is the mindfulness challenge.

What are some cognitive distortions at play in your scrupulosity OCD?

_____

_____

Practice: Try doing some automatic thought records on situations that trigger your scrupulosity OCD. See the following sample automatic thought record.

Sample Automatic Thought Record

Trigger What set you off?	Automatic Thought What is the OCD saying?	Challenge What is an alternative to the distorted thinking?
Had a thought about a religious figure doing a sexual act.	Because I had this thought, I'm a sick, twisted person who doesn't belong in heaven.	I can't control what pops into my head, and it makes no sense to punish myself for something that's out of my control. In my experience I tend not to go out of my way to sexually fantasize about religious figures, and I have no evidence that what's going on in my mind is an indictment of who I am and what I believe. I will have to accept that I don't know how God interprets the awareness of these thoughts and stand up to the challenge of my OCD.

Action Tools for Scrupulosity OCD

It cannot be understated that mindfulness is an essential element of the way in which exposure and response prevention works. If you attempt to do exposure to a triggering picture but, all the while, tell yourself that you hate it, it's wrong, and everything will be just fine, you are essentially washing your hands while touching something dirty. You are resisting, not accepting, the fear experience. It's painful anyway, but without mindfully observing the urge to respond compulsively, it's pain without purpose. The thoughts may be sickening and insidiously creative, but your job is to watch them go by and demonstrate to your brain that they are not threats to you. If you want confidence in your faith, you have to show the mind that something as insignificant as thoughts and feelings shouldn't be calculated as having the power to dissuade you from confronting your fear.

In Vivo ERP for Scrupulosity OCD

Scrupulosity can become an obsession from a wide variety of angles, so the first thing you will need to do is consider what you are afraid of in more specific detail. For example, if you are Christian and are dealing with intrusive thoughts about the devil turning you away from God, then you will want to target your exposures in the direction of things that bring the devil concept to mind. Examples include:

- Writing "666" somewhere or making it the background to your desktop wallpaper

- Looking at artistic portrayals of the devil

- Watching movies where the devil is a character or theme

Regarding the issue of committing minor transgressions within your religion, this can be tricky. On one hand, it's smart to work with your spiritual advisor on what kind of transgressions might be forgiven by your higher power for the purpose of bettering your mental health. Many subscribe, in one way or another, to the Judeo-Christian biblical description of the body as a "temple," and because the brain is in the body, we have a responsibility to take care of our mental health. Letting OCD run the show is perhaps more sinful than letting yourself make mistakes. On the other hand, be wary of using your spiritual advisors primarily for the purpose of compulsive reassurance. Have them help you set guidelines, but ultimately it's your challenge to be willing to sit with your uncertainty about whether you are doing a poor job of following these guidelines.

For moral scrupulosity, you can construct your compulsive hierarchy around those things that you see others doing that appear to trigger you excessively. Examples may be:

- Allowing yourself to temporarily think negative thoughts about people

- Purposefully telling a small lie in which no one gets hurt but you know you are being dishonest (for example, saying you spent slightly more on something than you did)

- Purposefully putting a recyclable in the trash bin, pouring some leftover cooking grease down the kitchen sink, or allowing the faucet to run the whole time you brush your teeth

Remember that the goal here is not to become a "bad" person or lose the love of your higher power. The goal here is to live a life of your *own* values and commit to engaging in healthy behavior independently from OCD's intrusive demands.

Imaginal ERP for Scrupulosity OCD

A scrupulosity script can very easily be overwhelming for the religious scrupulosity sufferer and depressing for the moral scrupulosity sufferer. While this technique can be extremely effective, we encourage you to work on these scripts with the guidance of a treatment professional, if you can access one. On your own, start with an acceptance script (see the "Acceptance Scripts" section in chapter 3), acknowledging your obsessions and compulsions and reminding yourself of what you will need to accept when you fight back against the OCD.

The scrupulosity script starts by your admitting (falsely) that you are not the decent human being you want to be and that your thoughts and feelings define who you are. You then follow with a statement about the consequences that come from this admission and how you and your loved ones are affected. This may mean describing horrific punishments, either on earth or in the afterlife. Here are some guiding questions:

What will you fail to do in the pious or morally responsible way?

_____

_____

How will you feel knowing that you are responsible for this bad choice?

_____

_____

How will others be affected by your bad choice?

_____

_____

What other decisions will you make throughout the rest of your life because of your failure?

_____

_____

How will these decisions bring about judgment (from your higher power or from society)?

_____

_____

How will you be punished in the end? Describe the punishment in detail.

_____

_____

Remember that the goal here is not to convince you that your fear is true. The goal is to make contact with the thoughts, feelings, and physical sensations that come with your obsession and mindfully stay in contact with them, for however long it takes to habituate. Without the OCD pressing the "meaning button," you can always find your way back to the present.

CHAPTER 14

Hyperawareness OCD

The underlying theme behind hyperawareness obsessions is *I am consciously aware of something benign that no one overtly thinks about, and I want to stop being aware of it, but I can't.* One way in which you may be looking at the nature of these obsessions is almost as *too much* mindfulness. In other words, it's an obsession *with* mindfulness, with attention to the present moment. However, it's the resistance to this awareness that actually pulls you away from the experience of the present moment, and it's thus *not* "mindfulness gone wild." It's just OCD attacking from another angle. Mindful acceptance must include acceptance of any discomfort that comes with awareness of the present moment. Instead of pulling away from the experience of awareness, mindfulness asks you to stay with it, whatever thoughts, feelings, or sensations may tag along.

Somatic obsessions (sometimes called *sensorimotor* or *somatoform* obsessions) deal with the intrusive sense of awareness of involuntary bodily processes, typically involving but not limited to:

- Awareness of breathing

- Awareness of blinking

- Awareness of swallowing

- Awareness of body positioning (for example, where your arms are in relation to the rest of your body)

- Awareness of physical sensations that are benign or of unknown origin (for example, itching, warmth, heartbeat, and so on)

- Awareness of ringing in the ears

- Awareness of eye "floaters"

Some additional common triggers in the category of hyperawareness include concern with:

- Awareness of benign sounds (for example, birds, wind chimes, traffic noises)

- Awareness of remembering songs (getting songs stuck in your head, sometimes called "earworms")

- Awareness of memories of specific images (sometimes benign, sometimes disturbing, but in either case involving a sense of being stuck with them)

- Awareness of your own thinking process, that you have a mind, that thinking is happening at a level that feels burdensome

What types of things do you find yourself hyperaware of that may cause you discomfort?

_____

_____

_____

_____

The primary obsessions associated with hyperawareness are:

- *I will never go back to doing these things involuntarily, and will therefore do them in a stilted or strange way.*

- *My awareness of this thing will become so burdensome that I won't be able to function, and will become depressed or go insane.*

What types of fears come up for you when you struggle to accept your awareness of these types of triggers?

_____

_____

_____

The primary compulsions associated with hyperawareness obsessions typically involve:

- Mental checking for the trigger (breath, swallowing, and so on)

- Mental review of the voluntary or involuntary nature of the trigger

- Mental review of the significance of the awareness

- Reassurance seeking (particularly from treatment providers) to confirm that this is not the sign of a severe mental illness, and that it will go away in a specific amount of time

- Avoidance of situations that might trigger the obsession (for example, avoiding parks due to bird noises, avoiding social interactions where hyperawareness may be upsetting)

What compulsions do you think you may be engaging in to resist accepting your hyperawareness trigger?

_____

_____

_____

_____

Acceptance Tools for Hyperawareness OCD

Perhaps more so here than in any other kind of OCD, mindfulness is the key way to alleviate hyperawareness obsessions. The greatest exposure for this type of obsession is acceptance. It's as if the OCD has opened a window to a view where you were previously unaware there was a window or a view. Resisting what you are seeing in this window and resisting the *presence* of the window only makes it bigger and more anxiety producing. This doesn't mean resigning yourself to *thinking* about your obsession for all time. To the contrary, the act of thinking or analyzing is counter to the experience of accepting thoughts as they come and go.

The problem inherent in these obsessions is not simply noticing the presence of the obsession. It's noticing the *noticing* and then resisting *that* experience. Acceptance in this form of OCD asks that we do exactly that, let go of fighting the noticing of the noticing. This means observing disturbing thoughts like *I may never swallow without thinking about it again, I'll always find my thought process burdensome,* or *I'll always be bothered by this sound.*

Hyperawareness of Thinking vs. Hearing Your Thoughts

When OCD attacks your very awareness, it can be terribly frightening. The only way to describe your experience is that you are "hearing" your thoughts or that they are "too loud." An untrained therapist may confuse this with auditory hallucinations and suggest a schizophrenia diagnosis. This couldn't be further from the truth. Hyperawareness of your thoughts is not the same thing as hearing voices. In auditory hallucinations, there's measurable activity in the auditory portion of the brain. The voices are *heard* in the same way that you hear sounds from the outside. Awareness of your inner voice is not the same thing as recording your thoughts into an audio-recording device and listening to them (in the way that some imaginal exposure is done). Although the experience may *feel* like the sound of your voice, the presence of intrusive thoughts must never be confused with the presence of auditory hallucinations. The short version is you're not crazy. You just have a brighter light shining on the idea that you are *thinking* than someone without OCD might have.

Practice: What thoughts, feelings, physical sensations, or other internal data do you believe you will need to mindfully accept as you alleviate your hyperawareness OCD?

_____

_____

Meditation Tips for Hyperawareness OCD

Meditation in the moment, and in specific meditative practice, may play a significant role in treating your hyperawareness obsession, even if you have an obsession with awareness of your breathing. In any form of meditation, you are working on strengthening the mental muscle that allows you to disengage from *thinking* and return to the present experience of the breath (or the stairs, the food, or whatever present thing is your anchor in the meditation session). When you focus on your breath, you may notice thoughts about whether you are attending to the present or *overattending*. Take note of *that* thought. Acknowledge that your mind has taken the act of meditation and shifted it to a performance review. Practice willingness to have that experience, and bring yourself back to the breath even if that seems like playing into the OCD. *I'm thinking about my breathing. I can accept that this thinking is happening and disengage from being an active participant in it. Even now I am participating by identifying it, but it's okay for me to be imperfect in this moment. Let me just take my time and let go of any problem solving I'm able to let go of in this moment. What if the thinking never stops? That's another thought. I can have that thought, not mind having it for now, and return to the breath.*

Assessment Tools for Hyperawareness OCD

The primary distorted thought in this form of OCD is that the experience of awareness is intolerable, that it won't end, and that it will eventually destroy the enjoyment of life itself. As such, the primary cognitive distortions are typically magnification of the thought, catastrophizing about an intolerable future, and "should" or "must" statements about what you believe you are supposed to be aware of or unaware of. Remember that cognitive restructuring is a backup tool, a device for you to use to aid in your struggle to disengage from compulsions and return to the present. Too much emphasis on cognitive restructuring as your primary approach to treatment can easily become a tool for more mental ritualizing, so use it sparingly.

What cognitive distortions are at play in your hyperawareness OCD?

_____

_____

Practice: Try doing some automatic thought records on situations that trigger your hyperawareness OCD. See the following sample automatic thought record.

Sample Automatic Thought Record

Trigger What set you off?	Automatic Thought What is the OCD saying?	Challenge What is an alternative to the distorted thinking?
Started thinking about my blinking.	I'm not blinking normally, because I'm thinking about it. So I must decide if I should blink more or less than I'm currently blinking to avoid looking odd.	It's not important how or when I blink, and I have no way of knowing if other people perceive it as normal or abnormal. I blink when I blink, and I have to accept that it sometimes makes me feel uncomfortable. It's only a problem to be aware of my blinking if I choose to respond to it as a problem.

Action Tools for Hyperawareness OCD

You may feel frustrated that you don't see yourself as doing compulsions, and the wrong treatment provider may confirm this fear if he or she is unfamiliar with mental rituals in OCD. But if you are responding to your thoughts, feelings, and sensations as if they aren't supposed to be there, then you are acting on a compulsion.

In Vivo ERP for Hyperawareness OCD

In vivo ERP for hyperawareness means eliminating avoidance of triggers, and instead going out of your way to purposefully *think* the thoughts instead of flee from them. As in other forms of OCD, there are several strategies, particularly avoidance and mental review, that involve compulsively resisting your awareness of an unwanted thought. You may have come to believe that the unwanted thought is inescapable because something like breathing, blinking, or thinking is essentially normal, whereas you may see thoughts of violence or fear of contamination as being somehow different. But the obsession here is not with the blinking, swallowing, and so on. It's with the fear that your *awareness* will keep you from experiencing joy or will make you descend into madness. So in essence, it's a fear of *mind contamination*. As such, anything you do to *cleanse* your mind of this fear should be viewed as a compulsion. So exposure therapy means purposefully putting yourself in situations where you may be especially hyperaware, and then resisting the mental review or avoidant impulses that follow.

For hyperawareness of thinking, try to engage in social interactions that may require some additional mental processing, such as ordering food from a menu. As you look at the menu, tell yourself that you have no idea what you will order, and try to hold on to the idea that there's too much information in front of you. Wait for the server to arrive, and then randomly pick an item at the last minute, risking being completely wrong.

For hyperawareness of breathing, purposefully meditate on your breath. When you begin to notice that you are *noticing* your breath more than you would like, tell yourself that this is absolutely terrible and will result in insanity. Note, this is a completely different process from actual mindful meditation, in which you would notice the thought about your breathing, acknowledge that it's okay for it to be there, and then let the thought flow through you without judgment. The purpose of this *exposure* form of meditation is to generate and habituate to the anxiety that comes with your fear. For hyperawareness of swallowing or blinking, you may practice swallowing while telling yourself you are doing it wrong. Doing this in public may heighten the anxiety.

Imaginal ERP for Hyperawareness OCD

It might be a good idea to start with an acceptance script for hyperawareness, something you can check in with once a day to point you in the right direction (see the "Acceptance Scripts" section in chapter 3). The key to your acceptance script should involve identifying specifically what your obsession is. Remember, it's not just the words—the content of your intrusive thought—but what you think having never-ending awareness of that content would *do* to you. Once you have identified the obsession, acknowledge the things you do to reassure yourself, or to try to make the obsession go away. Take a look at some of the mental compulsions you may be engaging in, or any other way in which you resist the presence of these thoughts.

The key to a good imaginal ERP script about hyperawareness is identifying what you are really afraid of. Try to answer the following questions to develop your script:

What will you be thinking about forever?

_____

_____

What makes this never-ending awareness intolerable or unacceptable?

_____

_____

How is it different from what "normal" people experience?

_____

_____

If the obsession continues for a very long time, what will be your strategy for addressing it?

_____

_____

If this strategy fails, what will happen to your mental stability when you discover that this obsession will never go away?

_____

What are a few things that would happen before you would no longer be able to function in society?

_____

How do the people you care about deal with this?

_____

_____

How will you end up?

_____

_____

It's absolutely fine if you don't feel ready to take this particular journey right now. If you've been struggling with this obsession, you've probably been spending a lot of effort trying *not* to go to the dark place where these questions have upsetting answers. Work on eliminating reassurance-seeking behaviors and avoidance first. Continue to read about and practice mindfulness skills. When you are ready to make more direct contact with your fear, you'll know.

Take a Breather

You've been through a lot. If you read through part 1, you took in a lot of information about what mindfulness is and how it's used alongside cognitive behavioral therapy to treat OCD. If you read all the chapters of part 2, just the chapters that you think would apply directly to you, or only one chapter related to your OCD, you made a huge step in taking back control of your life. Don't be discouraged if you found the suggestions for mindful acceptance, cognitive therapy, or exposure therapy too challenging just now. If you are working with a therapist, let this person know that you need to be guided through this process at a pace that you can tolerate. If you are going through this workbook on your own, then be your *own* therapist here, and reflect back to yourself that this is hard; there's no race to beat this disorder, and no prize for suffering the most.

If you are doing the practices but are struggling, go back to part 1 and review the larger concepts. Or take a break and come back when you're ready to sit with the inherent discomfort of fighting OCD this way. If you aren't doing the practices but are just reading this book to build the strength to take the next step, that's absolutely fine. Know your enemy. Attack when the battle strategy is clear.

PART 3

Mindfulness, OCD, and You

So far the focus of this workbook has been on you and your OCD, but few of us live in such a vacuum that the disorder affects only the way we think, feel, or sense internally. The outside world, the people we love, the work we do, the support we seek, and the way we seek it are all affected by the OCD. In this part of the book, we hope to explore the challenges inherent in living with OCD, communicating about OCD, and getting help for OCD, as well as how mindfulness can enhance success in these areas.

CHAPTER 15

Sharing Your OCD Experience

People notice. They may not know they're noticing, but if you suffer from OCD and spend any significant amount of time around other people, you've probably been asked some uncomfortable questions. That likely says a lot about the asker, but people have the hardest time containing their curiosity when it comes to seeing someone being compulsive. Maybe they notice that you use a lot of soap or take a long time before leaving the house. Or maybe they just notice that you seem to be *in your head* a lot. "What are you thinking about?" they may inquire. "What's wrong?" Oh, the look on their faces if you were to tell them the truth!

What Do People See?

Consider for a moment the ways in which people may be aware of your OCD. Even reading this last sentence, you may initially have an urge to start personalizing and mind reading. *Do people notice my OCD? Are they thinking terrible things?* Notice that your mind dived first in that direction, the one that involves judgment and labeling. Now try to come back and just focus on the external. What do people actually *see?* Do they see you shut down in conversations when you become uncomfortable? Do they see you skip over the first paper cup at the self-serve counter of the convenience store to get the second, *cleaner* one? Do they see you arriving late for work? If people see anything different about you because of the OCD, what might it be? Write it here:

_____

_____

_____

_____

When someone asks about your behavior, the feelings this arouses in you may largely depend on the way in which you are asked. What's the way you would least want to be asked about your OCD?

_____

_____

How would it make you feel?

_____

_____

If having your OCD be ignored weren't an option, how would you most prefer to be asked about it?

_____

_____

What types of feelings do you think this experience might make you aware of?

_____

_____

Mindfulness is often about separating what things *are* from what you believe they could mean. Taking note of your previous responses can help identify the difference between how the outside world perceives your OCD, and what you think others' perceptions mean about you.

Who Gets to Know?

OCD is a common mental health issue, and as such it makes little sense to treat it, and yourself, like some sort of strange, unknowable thing. Furthermore, treating your OCD like a character flaw instead of the clinical issue that it really is can be an impediment to treatment. So part of looking at your OCD clinically necessitates sharing about it as if it were, mindfully speaking, just a thing.

Advantages and Disadvantages of Sharing

The advantages of sharing your OCD with others are:

- It may bring a close relationship closer.

- It may be relevant to specific accommodations at work or school.

- It may make it easier to tolerate thoughts and feelings about secrecy (beware of compulsive confessing, though).

- It may ease your process of finding appropriate help.

What potential advantages do you see in disclosing information about your OCD, and who do you think has earned this disclosure?

_____

_____

The disadvantages of sharing your OCD with others are:

- It may complicate a relationship, if the other person has difficulty accepting or understanding the disorder.

- It may reveal prejudices at work or school.

- It may be fodder for obsessing about what was disclosed.

- It may complicate issues with health insurance.

What potential disadvantages do you see in disclosing your OCD, and who in your life do you think has *not* earned this disclosure?

_____

_____

_____

Notice that the last two questions we posed use the word "potential," meaning that there's a fair amount of uncertainty to accept regarding what to share and with whom. While the previous questions may help you make an educated guess, you will still have to sit with the presence of discomfort that comes with knowing that your educated guess is still a guess. Try to remember that this discomfort is normal and expected when you are opening up about OCD.

"What's Your OCD?"

"What's your OCD?" is a profoundly personal question and one that you are likely to hear as the immediate follow-up to your revealing that you have OCD. If someone told you that he had irritable bowel syndrome, the polite response would be something along the lines of, "Oh, that must be hard to deal with." You certainly wouldn't dive straight into, "How many times a day do you have to run to the toilet?" But something about OCD, maybe the way it's portrayed in the media, makes the average nonsufferer feel somehow entitled to know what "kind" of OCD you have and what things you do. Just remember that this probably isn't meant to offend you. It likely comes from ignorance, not malevolence.

Explaining How You Think

If you choose to talk about your OCD, be aware of cognitive distortions that may creep in. For example, you may be thinking that you must describe your OCD *perfectly*. You don't have to do *anything* perfectly, so long as you are willing to sit with the feeling of its being less than perfect. You may be catastrophizing the response from the person you are sharing with. But you don't know what her response will be or what thoughts and feelings that response will bring about in you. You may notice some mind reading and personalizing getting in the way, that you assume that the person with whom you are sharing is thinking something in particular about you and your OCD.

Take a moment to review the "Challenging Cognitive Distortions" section in chapter 2. Which ones do you think may be a factor in your decision to share about your OCD?

_____

_____

_____

_____

There's no perfect way to describe your OCD to someone. Here are some ideas:

"I get stuck on certain details about things, and I play them over and over until they seem really important; then I have difficulty moving on from them."

"My brain is highly attuned to potential risks from certain things, and it makes me really want to avoid them and be sure I haven't come in contact with them."

"Sometimes my mind gets flooded with thoughts about not being the kind of person I want to be, and it makes me really uncomfortable. So I spend a lot of time trying to make things seem right to me, and it takes a lot of energy."

Notice how none of the previous examples requires any disclosure of the actual content of your thoughts. That level of disclosure is up to you, not the person who is asking. Use the following space to write some ideas for ways in which you can describe your OCD without having to let someone into the most private corridors of your mind:

_____

_____

_____

_____

Getting It

You may have shared about your OCD with friends, coworkers, or loved ones, and found yourself somewhat relieved and dissatisfied at the same time. You may feel that your partner or someone you care about simply doesn't *get* it. Sometimes this is a reflection of the fact that the nonsufferer on the receiving end of the disclosure has preconceived beliefs about mental health that block him from being open to any new information that conflicts with his philosophy. In other words, he doesn't *want* to get it.

But what's more common is that a loved one or an important person in your life hears it, reports fully understanding, and yet still struggles to fully accept it. She says, *Yeah, but if you know you're not supposed to do compulsions and you know that the thing you're afraid of is just an obsession, why not just stop doing compulsions?* This statement is a cry for help from the nonsufferer to better understand the OCD thought process, but the OCD sufferer often perceives this as an attack and another example of how isolating the disorder can be.

The truth is, if she doesn't have OCD, consider that maybe she doesn't really get it. But then she doesn't really *have* to either. Living with OCD is all about learning to mindfully accept this struggle with uncertainty. You don't need to be 100 percent certain that your hands are clean or your thoughts are safe. So you don't need someone outside of your head to understand you 100 percent; 80 percent is plenty, and it may be all that the person has the capacity to understand. This is okay.

You may understand only 80 percent of what the *other person* goes through. Whether it's your significant other or your best friend, there are lots of ways in which you connect only 80 percent but still feel fully connected. Take a moment to consider what you believe is absolutely necessary for the person closest to you to understand about your OCD. Here are some ideas:

I would never hurt my loved one despite what thoughts my OCD may present me with.

I'm as afraid of my trigger as my loved one is of his worst fear.

I can be trusted.

I am not insane.

For the person you *most* want to understand your OCD, what do you need to feel confident that she or he gets?

_____

_____

Mindfulness in this area means observing that you have thoughts and feelings of not being fully understood, as well as observing the urge to close that gap coming from your OCD. It's fine to let the gap remain, even if just for the exposure to your discomfort.

CHAPTER 16

Mindfulness and Staying on Track

Because OCD is a chronic condition, the endgame for mastering it means mastering your skills for managing the disorder. There's no cure for OCD. By definition, it is a disorder, and thus an exaggerated experience of a normal process. Unwanted thoughts, feelings, and physical sensations are normal events. The urge to avoid them is a normal urge. The strategies we employ to escape them, however compulsive, are typically normal behaviors. It's being *locked* into the obsessive-compulsive cycle and having this vicious circle grossly impair your functioning that makes OCD a disorder. It's not the simple presence of these normal events.

Mindfulness is a major tool in the arsenal against OCD symptoms. Combined with cognitive and behavioral therapy techniques, it's a skill set that you can expect to hone throughout your life, just as a martial arts master continues to train even after acquiring the highest possible belt. You can be a black belt in the MBCBT arts, but that includes adopting the philosophy of never giving up. It means looking at the goal as indefinite improvement—as a lifestyle shift, not a crash diet.

Like other chronic conditions, it will wax and wane throughout your life. But there are a few factors that are likely to increase your OCD's power over you and decrease your resolve to fight it. These are called *stressors*. Knowing what stressors exacerbate your OCD allows you to be prepared for the change in intensity of your symptoms, and to employ mindfulness and CBT skills before you get overwhelmed.

Stress Itself

Above all, nothing exacerbates OCD as much as simple, old-fashioned stress. Stress may be caused by the disorder itself or by your perception of events around you; but it's also often caused by the basic reality that we live in stressful times and take on stressful responsibilities. If you are working long hours, if you are a parent or caretaker, if you have financial difficulties, if you have medical issues—*any* of these things and more can bring about this experience that we call "stress."

If what's expected of us is what we can handle, we see it as *acceptable* stress. If it's more than what we believe we can handle, we handle it anyway but call it *unacceptable* stress. When you are stressed, you will experience more intrusive thinking, more compulsive urges, and more of a desire to avoid and self-soothe. What things in your life, besides the presence of OCD itself, cause you stress?

_____

_____

_____

_____

_____

Know that when these things are occurring, you can use the same MBCBT skills to help manage and accept your experience of stress. If any of these stressors is within your power to change, then change it through direct action. That will often be more effective than simply trying to cope with it. This may involve cutting back on work hours, returning fewer phone calls, or asking for more help with child care, for example. Know that when you remove stressors from your life, you may feel guilt, a sense of inadequacy, or concern about letting others down. Use mindfulness to allow for these thoughts and feelings so that they don't become stressors themselves.

What are some thoughts and feelings that come up for you when you consider reducing the stressors in your life?

_____

_____

Above all, the thing to remember when stress exacerbates your OCD is that the increase in the volume of mental noise in your disorder is not an indicator of the importance of the thoughts you are having. If, during a stressful time, you notice that you are washing your hands more, checking the locks more, ruminating on sexual or violent obsessions more, remember that this has no correlation to how dirty, unsafe, or threatening these triggers are. Your experience of your obsession is simply being distorted by the exacerbation of your disorder. Let yourself see that it's being distorted and remind yourself, *Things are the same as they were before. I'm just more sensitive to my triggers because of stress. I still have to accept uncertainty, and I still have to resist feeding my OCD with compulsive behavior.*

Hormonal Changes for Women with OCD

Nienke Vulink and colleagues (2006) found a likely correlation between hormonal changes in women and an exacerbation of OCD symptoms. Menstruation (including premenstruation), menopause, and pregnancy were all found to include increased symptoms (although some study participants reported reduced symptoms during pregnancy). We have seen many female clients enter the office completely overwhelmed and deflated by what they see as a sudden, irreversible relapse of the disorder, as if all the work they had put into getting better were pointless. After a long discussion about how hard it is to live with OCD, how challenging it is to treat your OCD, and what bravery it takes to stand up to this terrible disorder, the session ends with, "Oh, and I'm on my period too!" Likewise, we have treated many women whose OCD symptoms were dramatically exacerbated either during or immediately after pregnancy, with obsessional symptoms most frequently focused on the fear of harming the newborn.

Some women are more sensitive to hormonal changes than others, but if you notice an increase in your OCD, particularly if it coincides with pregnancy or your monthly cycle, then you can take the opportunity to get into mindfulness mode before the storm hits. If you know all the while that you are more sensitive to your triggers because of hormonal changes that are taking place, you can mindfully return to that concept each time. You can see the OCD not as a monster returning, but as just another symptom of this bodily experience that you have when your hormones shift.

Don't slip into self-punishment mode here. Don't criticize yourself for feeling weak, for not wanting to fight the OCD while a war goes on inside your body. Instead, let the volume of your thoughts and feelings go up and down without your actively participating in adjusting the volume knob. Just watch it do its thing, and remember that this, too, shall pass.

Maladaptive Coping Strategies

Mindfulness is the art of embracing things as they are. It's changing yourself by accepting yourself. It's a living paradox. To be mindful is to be open to reality as it is. But reality involves pain, intrusive thoughts, fear, and doubt. For you, reality involves having OCD. What this means is that states of *unreality* are the opposite of mindfulness. At certain doses, alcohol, other drugs, and pornography all have the appeal of escape to unreality. This doesn't mean that they are all bad at all doses or for all people. But if the process is one of avoidance, then it's counterindicative to treating your OCD.

Sometimes the things we do to feel better, to escape reality when it's uncomfortable, become sources of discomfort and stress themselves. Tempting as they may be, these moments of silence you can achieve by forcing massive doses of *unreality* on your mind only embolden the OCD. The escape sends the very clear message that the present reality is *not* tolerable. So while you may enjoy the high you get from whatever source of unreality you choose, the OCD will wait for your return and will remind you of why you left.

Still, not all escape is bad or destructive. Sometimes, temporarily leaving can be a shift to a positive, adaptive place, and returning can bring about a healthier perspective. A vacation or a strenuous workout can also be a form of walking away from stress. And not all escape has to be particularly meaningful either. Escaping into your favorite TV show or video game for a bit can be a healthy, positive reward for staying in reality all day. It may be necessary for you to assess, perhaps with the help of a loved one or a treatment provider, what forms of escape are adaptive and what forms are destructive.

If you are struggling with an addiction of any kind, it's important to get help and treat that alongside (if not before) working on your OCD. While one may exacerbate the other, addiction is its own beast and often requires its own treatment strategies.

What are some adaptive ways in which you escape that add value to your life?

_____

_____

What are some destructive ways of escape that may be more trouble than they're worth?

_____

_____

Other Stressors

Other stressors that can exacerbate OCD may include:

- Other mental health issues (for example, depression, bipolar disorder, or personality disorders)

- Insomnia or other sleep issues

- Family issues

- Work issues

- Financial issues

- Medical health issues

What are the stressors in your life that appear to correlate with an increase in your OCD symptoms?

_____

_____

_____

What mindfulness concepts would be useful to remember when you become aware that these stressors are exacerbating your OCD?

_____

_____

_____

_____

Lapses vs. Relapses

Being perfect is not a reasonable goal for anyone. Perfectly mastering mindfulness and CBT skills won't result in the total absence of all unwanted experiences. If you try, if you invest in doing MBCBT to treat your disorder, then you are likely to vastly improve the quality of your life. But you will stumble along the way. You will think to yourself, *I got this*, and then you will walk right into a metaphorical spiderweb of OCD. As you scramble to figure out what compulsions you have to do in order to feel certain that no spider has bitten you, you may become aware of the fact that you have completely stopped following your own MBCBT advice. How you frame this awareness from this point forward will have a profound impact on how long you spend anguishing in the service of your OCD.

A Lapse Is Not a Relapse

You don't start over from square one every time you act on a compulsion. Success in managing your OCD is largely measured by the decrease in frequency and significance of compulsive behaviors. If you've managed to resist double-checking the stove for a week and then one morning you decided to go back and check a second or third time, this doesn't render that week of progress obsolete. If you've resisted seeking reassurance from your partner about your obsessive thoughts for two weeks and then one day you find the words, "Can I just ask you one thing?" spilling from your lips, this is not an indication of your failure to beat OCD.

Fill out an automatic thought record to challenge distorted thinking that might be going on regarding setbacks. For example, imagine that you have been working on resisting the urge to compulsively check to see if you left the stove on. Then, a life stressor shows up, and your ability to tolerate discomfort feels compromised. You know you need to be strong and resist, but you just don't have the strength today, so you end up going back to an old, familiar way of doing things.

Sample Automatic Thought Record

Trigger What set you off?	Automatic Thought What is the OCD saying?	Challenge What is an alternative to the distorted thinking?
Started excessive checking of stove again.	Because I had been doing better and now I'm back to checking again, I'm a failure and I'll never get a handle on this OCD.	It would benefit me to more carefully monitor these urges while I'm under this extra stress. Self-punishing won't help me stay on top of the OCD. I'm having a hard time.
Surprisingly high anxiety after seeing horror movie.	I should be over this after all the ERP work I did. I'm going to start obsessing about harm again, and this time I won't be able to handle it.	I don't know what's going to happen in the future. Spikes happen from time to time, and it's been a while since I got triggered like this. So I appear to be doing well overall. If I need to do more exposure work, I can check in with my therapist for a booster session. Horror movies are supposed to trigger you sometimes!

Mindfulness for OCD necessitates looking at the bigger picture. The bigger picture in treating OCD is a bumpy trail up a mountain. You have to be willing to slip on rocks, scrape your knee, and even slide downward from time to time. Lapses are teaching moments. You want to get to a place where you can say, *Good one, OCD, ya got me.* Then you can remember how to be prepared for whatever got you into this place where you chose compulsions over the tolerance of uncertainty.

CHAPTER 17

Getting Help

If you're reading this book, you probably came to the conclusion that something wasn't working right for you. Maybe you already knew you had OCD, or maybe you were just curious about why you felt plagued by unwanted thoughts and feelings and thought giving it the name "OCD" would help. It's likely that you came to the conclusion that you wanted to do something about this problem, whether you want to label it a "mental health challenge" or just a way of living that you're ready to change. This is a self-help book, so clearly you're a self-starter of some sort. We believe that implementing the tools we've discussed so far will not only alleviate your symptoms, but also change your perspective on having OCD altogether. That being said, we cannot overstate the value of working with an OCD specialist trained in mindfulness-based cognitive behavioral therapy. Learning to be your own nonjudgmental observer is a mighty feat. Having a trained, competent therapist *start* from that position of being a nonjudgmental observer *for* you can be a tremendous asset.

It's scary to ask for help. The OCD mind is likely to frame that as some sort of weakness. It can blind you to the reality that being able to recognize when, where, and how to get help is actually a sign of strength! But this is your life we're talking about here. So whether we're talking about a psychiatrist who will manage your medication needs or a cognitive behavioral therapist who will direct your treatment program, you're asking someone to participate in changing your brain chemistry and your perspective on the mind. It's a thing of great value, and that means that it matters whom you choose and what this professional does.

If you are uncomfortable about the idea of getting professional help for your OCD, what are some of the thoughts and feelings you notice coming up at this moment?

_____

_____

_____

_____

_____

_____

Where to Begin

Different therapeutic modalities have different assets and weaknesses, but the best understood, best researched, and most effective treatment for obsessive-compulsive disorder is cognitive behavioral therapy. The most direct way to find an OCD specialist in your area is to visit www.ocfoundation.org/treatment_providers.aspx and type in your search parameters. The International OCD Foundation (IOCDF) is the largest nonprofit organization devoted to the OCD community, and has a vast amount of credible resources. If you have difficulty finding a local OCD specialist, see if there's one you can work with online or via telephone. You may also be interested in seeking any group or intensive treatment options that are available.

If there are no specialists accessible to you on the IOCDF registry, you may wish to see who is available in your area through other search mechanisms, but be sure to ask professionals about their experience with treating OCD.

What You Need to Ask

When you call a therapist, you first need to ask the person how much experience he has with OCD, or how much of his practice is devoted to the treatment of OCD. Many therapists include obsessive-compulsive disorder as part of a long list of things they can treat, but they may not be familiar enough with the disorder to implement it in the most effective way. Be especially sure to ask professionals about exposure with response prevention. There's no treatment for OCD without ERP.

When to Run

OCD specialists talk a lot. They ask a lot of questions. They are oriented on the treatment of the OCD and the objectives that need to be met to achieve your goals. They teach the treatment concepts, they assign homework, and they review the work. They help you do the work right there in the office when possible. Any therapist who encourages you to simply "talk it out" or "free-associate" is not only wasting your money, but also may be encouraging you to do more compulsions.

In short, the treatment cannot be focused on a deeper analysis of *why* you are having the thoughts and feelings that you are having. You don't need to get to the root of anything or reveal your secret identity. While some analysis may be of some use down the road and may reveal some valuable insights about your sense of self, it won't help you turn the tables on your OCD. To the contrary, it will only make you think harder. If you're seeking treatment for your OCD, you have done plenty of thinking already. Demand to be put to work!

Additional Mindfulness Training

If you are doing self-help using this workbook and other books, or if you are working with an OCD specialist, it may also be of benefit to do some additional mindfulness training outside of your therapy. There are a variety of institutions that provide mindfulness seminars, meditation retreats, and other tools for expanding your understanding of mindfulness. Reading about and practicing mindfulness in general will contribute positively to your fight against OCD.

Take a Big Breather

You've taken in a lot of information. To be present with this book necessarily involved being present with some of your most unwanted thoughts and feelings. Hopefully there were also times when you felt at ease, relieved, and inspired for your future. Give yourself a pat on the back; you deserve recognition. What works about this phrase in this particular moment is that it implies that you can give something to yourself. It implies that you can see yourself and offer up recognition, support, and kindness. Give yourself a "pat on the back" for doing as well as you do in life, despite your struggle with OCD, and for taking a step in a healthy direction.

Immediately after you finish reading these last words, you may notice an urge to go back through the book, reexamine some of its content, and think especially hard about what it means *to* you or *about* you. It's okay to have that urge, but perhaps you can take *this* opportunity to simply notice it for a moment.

Let the book end and let yourself off the hook for a few beats. You very likely have a lot of work ahead of you. You may be ready to contact a professional for treatment, hone your OCD-fighting skills, and charge the battlefield. Or you may be tired of the feeling of having to do something. It would be nice to just be okay for a second instead of always working on becoming better. So do nothing right now.

Sit with the feeling of wanting to do the hard work of fighting the OCD or wanting to stop dealing with it altogether, whatever is real for you in this moment. By choosing to sit for just these few beats and feel what you are feeling, it's inevitable: the work has already begun.

Resources

The list below represents a handful of books we have encountered along the way that contain especially valuable information. It is by no means an exhaustive list. There are many excellent books on OCD and on mindfulness. And no one book, including the one you are reading at this moment, is the definitive book on understanding OCD. This is due in part to the personal nature of the disorder. Who you are will influence how you connect with the material, so we recommend reading a lot of material on the subjects of OCD and mindfulness so that you have plenty of information to connect with.

OCD Books

Each book on OCD will have an angle on CBT treatment that's unique to the author. You may not resonate with every idea the author has about what OCD is and how to treat it. Try to take in each OCD book as if the reading were an exercise of its own. With each book, you are building a space in your mind for strengthening your larger understanding of the disorder and its treatment. You might notice that your OCD latches onto pieces of information that you don't like or that don't make sense to you. Don't insist on always understanding what you are reading as you read it. Practice exposure to whatever discomfort you may have, including the idea that you are not retaining enough of the best information in each book.

Baer, L. 2001. *Imp of the Mind: Exploring the Silent Epidemic of Obsessive Bad Thoughts*. New York: Dutton. This is an important book for understanding the nature of "bad" thoughts and why we have them. If you are struggling with obsessions of a violent or sexual nature, this is a must-read.

Grayson, J. 2003. *Freedom from Obsessive Compulsive Disorder: A Personalized Recovery Program for Living with Uncertainty.* New York: Jeremy P. Tarcher/Putnam. This book is an excellent self-help resource that carefully deconstructs the role of uncertainty in OCD and its treatment.

Hyman, B. M., and C. Pedrick. 2010. *The OCD Workbook: Your Guide to Breaking Free from Obsessive-Compulsive Disorder.* 3rd ed. Oakland, CA: New Harbinger Publications. This is an excellent self-help workbook with an emphasis on challenging distorted thinking and constructing effective hierarchies for behavioral therapy.

Osborn, I. 1998. *Tormenting Thoughts and Secret Rituals: The Hidden Epidemic of Obsessive-Compulsive Disorder.* New York: Pantheon Books. This book provides an excellent overview of OCD and its treatment, from both a historical and practical perspective.

Purdon, C., and D. A. Clark. 2005. *Overcoming Obsessive Thoughts: How to Gain Control of Your OCD.* Oakland, CA: New Harbinger Publications. Here you can find especially useful tools for challenging faulty appraisals of intrusive thoughts.

Schwartz, J. 1996. *Brain Lock: Free Yourself from Obsessive-Compulsive Behavior.* With B. Beyette. New York: ReganBooks. This book offers a comprehensive explanation of how OCD works in the brain.

These books represent a small sample, but for a truly comprehensive list of books on OCD, we recommend visiting www.ocfoundation.org/Books.aspx.

Mindfulness Books

We recommend always having one mindfulness book going. Keep it on your nightstand, for example. It doesn't have to be the main book you are reading. Mindfulness is not about linear thinking, so sitting and reading a mindfulness book cover to cover as you would read a novel might not be the best approach. Just read a little at a time. Chapters of mindfulness books tend to be very short, so you can literally devote a minute or two toward it each day and sit with the thoughts and feelings it stirs in you.

Reading about mindfulness is much like meditation itself. You may notice your OCD mind discounting a lot of what you see in these books, because it doesn't gel with your personal philosophy or is difficult to grasp. Let this happen. Don't be embarrassed if you think from time to time, *What is this person talking about?* Honestly attempt to take in something from each book. Over time, these insights will accumulate, and you will have your own evolving definition of mindfulness.

Here's a short list of mindfulness books that may be especially helpful:

Chödrön, P. 1991. *The Wisdom of No Escape: And the Path of Loving-Kindness.* 1st ed. Boston: Shambhala Publications. This is an excellent primer on mindfulness, acceptance, and the concept of "loving-kindness" toward oneself and the world.

Hayes, S. C. 2005. *Get Out of Your Mind and Into Your Life: The New Acceptance and Commitment Therapy.* With Sam Spencer. Oakland, CA: New Harbinger Publications. This workbook for acceptance and commitment therapy is an excellent tool for understanding mindfulness, the role of acceptance in well-being, and the pitfalls of avoidance.

Kabat-Zinn, J. 2005. *Wherever You Go, There You Are: Mindfulness Meditation in Everyday Life.* New York: Hyperion. This book focuses on mindful meditation and the value of staying present in daily life.

Nhat Hanh, Thich. 1987. *The Miracle of Mindfulness: A Manual on Meditation.* Rev. ed. Trans. by M. Ho, drawings by V.-D. Mai. Boston: Beacon Press. Here you can learn about meditation and mindfulness principles, and practice increasing your awareness.

Siegel, D. J. 2007. *The Mindful Brain: Reflection and Attunement in the Cultivation of Well-Being.* New York: W. W. Norton and Company. This book integrates the concepts of mindfulness with recent developments in the world of neuroscience research.

Tolle, E. 2004. *The Power of Now: A Guide to Spiritual Enlightenment.* Vancouver, BC: Namaste Publishing; Novato, CA: New World Library. This is an interesting exploration of the relationship between the mind and the observing self, with an emphasis on staying in the moment.

Online Resources

The Internet offers a wide variety of free support and information on OCD. The following is a very short list of sites on OCD, each of which features multiple resources and links:

International OCD Foundation (ocfoundation.org)

Beyond OCD (beyondocd.org)

OCD-UK (ocduk.org)

ADAA (adaa.org)

Discussion boards can also be excellent tools for learning about and getting support for the treatment of OCD. While there's an inherent risk in seeking and receiving reassurance in this format, the ability to write to others and remind yourself that you're not alone can be invaluable.

International OCD Foundation (www.ocfoundation.org/yahoo.aspx) features a comprehensive list of all active discussion boards.

OCD-Support (http://health.groups.yahoo.com/group/OCD-Support/) is a large OCD discussion group where you can get feedback from James Claiborn, Michael Jenike, and Jonathan Grayson on OCD issues, as well as support from fellow sufferers.

Pure O - OCD (http://healthy.groups.yahoo.com/group/pure_o_ocd) is a discussion board with an emphasis on HOCD, POCD, ROCD, and mental rituals in OCD.

References

Aardema, F., and K. O'Connor. 2007. "The Menace Within: Obsessions and the Self." *Journal of Cognitive Psychotherapy* 21 (3):182–97.

Abramowitz, J. S. 2006. "The Psychological Treatment of Obsessive-Compulsive Disorder." *Canadian Journal of Psychiatry* 51 (7):407–16.

Barrera, T. L., and P. J. Norton. 2011. "The Appraisal of Intrusive Thoughts in Relation to Obsessional-Compulsive Symptoms." *Cognitive Behaviour Therapy* 40 (2):98–110.

Bell, J. 2007. *Rewind, Replay, Repeat.* Center City, MN: Hazelden.

Bennett-Levy, J. 2003. "Mechanisms of Change in Cognitive Therapy: The Case of Automatic Thought Records and Behavioural Experiments." *Behavioural and Cognitive Psychotherapy* 31 (3):261–77.

Berman, N. C., J. S. Abramowitz, M. G. Wheaton, C. Pardue, and L. Fabricant. 2011. "Evaluation of an In Vivo Measure of Thought-Action Fusion." *Journal of Cognitive Psychotherapy* 25 (2):155–64.

Bloch, S. 2004. "A Pioneer in Psychotherapy Research: Aaron Beck." *Australian and New Zealand Journal of Psychiatry* 38 (11–12):855–67.

Brady, R. E., T. G. Adams, and J. M. Lohr. 2010. "Disgust in Contamination-Based Obsessive-Compulsive Disorder: A Review and Model." *Expert Review of Neurotherapeutics* 10 (8):1295–1305.

Cha, K. R., M.-S. Koo, C.-H. Kim, J. W. Kim, W.-J. Oh, H. S. Suh, and H. S. Lee. 2008. "Nonverbal Memory Dysfunction in Obsessive-Compulsive Disorder Patients with Checking Compulsions." *Depression and Anxiety* 25 (11):E115–20.

Chödrön, P. 1991. *The Wisdom of No Escape: And the Path of Loving-Kindness.* 1st ed. Boston: Shambhala Publications.

Ciarrocchi, J. W. 1995. *The Doubting Disease: Help for Scrupulosity and Religious Compulsions.* Mahwah, NJ: Paulist Press.

Clark, D. A. 2005. "Focus on 'Cognition' in Cognitive Behavior Therapy for OCD: Is It Really Necessary?" *Cognitive Behaviour Therapy* 34 (3):131–39.

Clark, R. E. 2004. "The Classical Origins of Pavlov's Conditioning." *Integrative Physiological and Behavioral Science* 39 (4):279–94.

Einstein, D. A., and R. G. Menzies. 2004. "Role of Magical Thinking in Obsessive-Compulsive Symptoms in an Undergraduate Sample." *Depression and Anxiety* 19 (3):174–79.

Fairfax, H. 2008. "The Use of Mindfulness in Obsessive Compulsive Disorder: Suggestions for Its Application and Integration in Existing Treatment." *Clinical Psychology and Psychotherapy* 15 (1):53–59.

Frost, R. O., and V. Hristova. 2011. "Assessment of Hoarding." *Journal of Clinical Psychology* 67 (5):456–66.

Hayes, S. C. 2005. *Get Out of Your Mind and Into Your Life: The New Acceptance and Commitment Therapy.* With S. Smith. Oakland, CA: New Harbinger Publications.

Houghton, S., D. Saxon, M. Bradburn, T. Ricketts, and G. Hardy. 2010. "The Effectiveness of Routinely Delivered Cognitive Behavioural Therapy for Obsessive-Compulsive Disorder: A Benchmarking Study." *British Journal of Clinical Psychology* 49 (4):473–89.

McCallie, M. S., C. M. Blum, and C. J. Hood. 2006. "Progressive Muscle Relaxation." *Journal of Human Behavior in the Social Environment* 13 (3):51–66.

Moritz, S., D. Jacobsen, B. Willenborg, L. Jelinek, and S. Fricke. 2006. "A Check on the Memory Deficit Hypothesis of Obsessive-Compulsive Checking." *European Archives of Psychiatry and Clinical Neuroscience* 256 (2):82–86.

Nickerson, R. S. 1998. "Confirmation Bias: A Ubiquitous Phenomenon in Many Guises." *Review of General Psychology* 2 (2):175–220.

Peck, M. S. 1978. *The Road Less Traveled: A New Psychology of Love, Traditional Values, and Spiritual Growth.* 1st ed. New York: Touchstone.

Rector, N. A., A. R. Daros, C. L. Bradbury, and M. A. Richter. 2012. "Disgust Recognition in Obsessive-Compulsive Disorder: Diagnostic Comparisons and Posttreatment Effects." *Canadian Journal of Psychiatry* 57 (3):177–83.

Ruscio, A. M., D. J. Stein, W. T. Chiu, and R. C. Kessler. 2010. "The Epidemiology of Obsessive-Compulsive Disorder in the National Comorbidity Survey Replication." *Molecular Psychiatry* 15 (1):53–63.

Saxena, S. D., E. Gorbis, J. O'Neill, S. K. Baker, M. A. Mandelkern, K. M. Maidment, S. Chang, N. Salamon, A. L. Brody, J. M. Schwartz, and E. D. London. 2009. "Rapid Effects of Brief Intensive Cognitive-Behavioral Therapy on Brain Glucose Metabolism in Obsessive-Compulsive Disorder: PET Study of Brief Intensive CBT for OCD." *Molecular Psychiatry* 14 (2):197–205.

Siegel, D. J. 2007. *The Mindful Brain: Reflection and Attunement in the Cultivation of Well-Being.* New York: W. W. Norton and Company.

Staddon, J. E. R., and D. T. Cerutti. 2003. "Operant Conditioning." *Annual Review of Psychology* 54 (1):115–44.

Vulink, N. C., D. Denys, L. Bus, and H. G. Westenberg. 2006. "Female Hormones Affect Symptom Severity in Obsessive-Compulsive Disorder." *International Clinical Psychopharmacology* 21 (3):171–75.

Weinrach, S. G. 1988. "Cognitive Therapist: A Dialogue with Aaron Beck." *Journal of Counseling and Development* 67 (3):154–64.

Williams, M. T., and S. G. Farris. 2011. "Sexual Orientation Obsessions in Obsessive-Compulsive Disorder: Prevalence and Correlates." *Psychiatry Research* 187 (1–2):156–59.

Williams, M. T., S. G. Farris, E. Turkheimer, A. Pinto, K. Ozanick, M. E. Franklin, M. Liebowitz, H. B. Simpson, and E. B. Foa. 2011. "Myth of the Pure Obsessional Type in Obsessive-Compulsive Disorder." *Depression and Anxiety* 28 (6):495–500.

Jon Hershfield, MFT, is a psychotherapist specializing in the treatment of obsessive compulsive disorder and related disorders using mindfulness-based cognitive behavioral therapy (MBCBT). He is also the associate director of the UCLA Child OCD Intensive Outpatient Program at Resnick Neuropsychiatric Hospital, moderator of a popular online discussion board devoted to fostering a better understanding of OCD with primarily mental rituals, a professional contributor to multiple online OCD forums, and a frequent presenter at the International Obsessive Compulsive Disorder Foundation's annual conference.

Tom Corboy, MFT, is the executive director of the OCD Center of Los Angeles, which he founded in 1999. He is a licensed psychotherapist specializing in MBCBT for the treatment of OCD and related anxiety-based conditions. In addition to his work with individual clients, he has trained and mentored many post-graduate interns, has presented at numerous conferences held by the International OCD Foundation (IOCDF), and has facilitated weekly therapy groups for adults with OCD since 1997.

Foreword writer **James Claiborn, PhD, ABPP,** is a psychologist in private practice specializing in OCD and related disorders. He is a diplomate of the American Board of Professional Psychology, and a diplomate and Founding Fellow of the Academy of Cognitive Therapy. He is a member of the Scientific Advisory Board of the International OCD Foundation and has presented internationally on OCD, cognitive behavioral therapy (CBT), and other topics.

FROM OUR PUBLISHER—

As the publisher at New Harbinger and a clinical psychologist since 1978, I know that emotional problems are best helped with evidence-based therapies. These are the treatments derived from scientific research (randomized controlled trials) that show what works. Whether these treatments are delivered by trained clinicians or found in a self-help book, they are designed to provide you with proven strategies to overcome your problem.

Therapies that aren't evidence-based—whether offered by clinicians or in books—are much less likely to help. In fact, therapies that aren't guided by science may not help you at all. That's why this New Harbinger book is based on scientific evidence that the treatment can relieve emotional pain.

This is important: if this book isn't enough, and you need the help of a skilled therapist, use the following resources to find a clinician trained in the evidence-based protocols appropriate for your problem. And if you need more support—a community that understands what you're going through and can show you ways to cope—resources for that are provided below, as well.

Real help is available for the problems you have been struggling with. The skills you can learn from evidence-based therapies will change your life.

Matthew McKay, PhD
Publisher, New Harbinger Publications

new harbinger
CELEBRATING
40 YEARS

**If you need a therapist, the following organization
can help you find a therapist trained in cognitive behavioral therapy (CBT).**

The Association for Behavioral & Cognitive Therapies (ABCT) Find-a-Therapist service offers a list of therapists schooled in CBT techniques. Therapists listed are licensed professionals who have met the membership requirements of ABCT and who have chosen to appear in the directory.
Please visit www.abct.org and click on *Find a Therapist*.

**For additional support for patients, family, and friends,
please contact the following:**

International OCD Foundation (IOCDF)
Visit www.ocfoundation.org

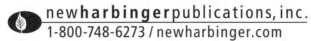